REEDS
MARIT
FLAG
HANDBOOK

Edited by
MIRANDA DELMAR-MORGAN

Based on *Reed's Maritime Flags*
by Sir Peter Johnson

Published by Adlard Coles Nautical
an imprint of A & C Black Publishers Ltd
38 Soho Square, London W1D 3HB
www.adlardcoles.com

Copyright © Miranda Delmar-Morgan 2006
Based on *Reed's Maritime Flags* © Sir Peter Johnson 2002

First edition 2006

ISBN 0-7136-7133-5
ISBN 9780-7136-7133-9

atural,
renewable and recyclable. The logging and manufacturing
processes conform to the environmental regulations of the
country of origin.

Typeset in Myriad 8/11 pt
Printed and bound in Singapore by Star Standard

Note: While all reasonable care has been taken in the
publication of this edition, the publisher takes no responsi-
bility for the use of the methods or products described in the
book.

CONTENTS

CONTENTS

AUTHOR'S NOTE

Flags are in use at sea by all kinds of vessel, from working ships to warships to yachts, both sail and power. There is a difference between the use of flags on land and at sea. Much of what follows in this book applies to flags wherever they are used afloat and also when hoisted on shore in a maritime connection. However, there is considerable emphasis on yachts and small working craft. Navies and shipping lines have their own regulations and practices and they are unlikely to need the advice given here. Yachts, motorboats and other small craft are, to some extent, on their own in this field. This little handbook is intended to provide their crews with a quick and ready reference for the use of flags at sea and on the shoreline.

There are technical implications to certain words in the English language used when flags, or *colours*, are shown. These words include *fly* and *wear*. Strictly speaking, a ship or boat wears a flag and the mariner flies a flag. Other terms such as *display*, *hoist*, *show*, and *rig* are also used but for easy reading they should be considered more or less interchangeable. The word 'yacht' here, unless specified, can be taken to mean either a sailing or motor yacht.

ACKNOWLEDGEMENTS

Grateful thanks are extended to Commander R Porteous RN; Warrant Officer 1(C) Dave Allport (Yeoman of The Admiralty); Graham Bartram of The Flag Institute; Michael A Faul, Editor of *Flag Master* magazine; Mike Weston, John Bazley and the librarians at the Warsash School of Maritime Studies; Natasha Brown at the International Maritime Organisation; and Darren Wall at the Institute of Maritime Law, University of Southampton.

WHAT IS A FLAG?

Flags have been in use for a very long time. The Romans hung textiles from crossbars and raised spears decorated with patterns and 'devices' and we have all been doing much the same ever since.

When Neil Armstrong landed on the moon, the first thing he did was to erect the Stars and Stripes. It is said that he even stiffened the top edge to stop it drooping on the windless planet. Nobody watching television anywhere on Earth could have been left in any doubt that (a) somebody had landed on the moon, and (b) judging by the flag, they were American. The flag crossed all language barriers.

So flags provide a picture – but not always a welcome one. Every so often a flag representing an invading nation is burned in the streets of an occupied territory. The images are flashed around the world and it is clear that the locals don't like the visitors. Flags can be loaded with significance and arouse strong passions.

In the UK in 1997, following the death of Diana, Princess of Wales, an outcry arose in the popular press that the royal standard above the monarch's residence should be flown at half mast. Other flags around the country had been half-masted. The authorities pointed out that the royal standard signifies the sovereign and is always flown fully hoisted. Even when a king or queen dies, the royal standard is not half-masted because, on the death of the monarch, he or she is instantly succeeded by his or her heir. The standard therefore immediately represents the new head of state. Such explanations fell on deaf ears with the tabloid press, which was determined to pursue this story. Quite a clever compromise was reached whereby a different flag (actually the Union flag) was hoisted on the mast which, until then, had displayed the royal standard. This second flag was then lowered to half mast instead and the royal standard, wilfully misunderstood by the people, was removed from the fray. This relatively recent, quite serious problem for the British monarchy shows that flags can still raise considerable emotion and anger.

Their usage and meaning varies, depending on whether or not they are ashore or afloat. When flags are shown at harbour offices, seamen's training schools, lifeboat houses and yacht clubs, the practice followed is, as far as practicable, the same as on board ship. Mostly flag etiquette has been laid down by one navy or another and small craft skippers, such as ourselves, have inherited it. Sometimes we use it and sometimes we don't. Some of it is a matter of etiquette, some of it is antiquated, but quite a lot of it is still in current use. More important though is that some flag lore has become enshrined in international law and if nothing else you do at least need to know your legal obligations.

Customs and traditions of the sea

Most flag use at sea is derived from custom and tradition. Sometimes it is voluntary, often it is vague. It varies from one country to another, and some countries get much more upset about their flags than others.

Professional ships have their own traditional usage. Yachts should consult almanacs or follow club rules. There are various flag websites (listed in the Appendix) and the Royal Yachting Association and Cruising Association are a mine of information for those going abroad. Generally, it is wise to avoid extraneous flags, pennants and ensigns. They are likely to be wrong, and others may strain to identify a signal that is meaningless. Other customs and traditions cover not only the flag itself, but also when, how, and where it is hoisted.

So this book is for those of you who don't really care very much what you fly, but sometimes need to know, and for those who do care what you fly and want to get it right.

● How a flag is made

Flags for use at sea are widely available from manufacturers, ship and yacht chandlers and websites. Special ensigns are usually ordered through their particular yacht club.

Seagoing flags are nowadays made of woven or knitted polyester, which dries quickly and is hard-wearing. The design is either dyed into the fabric then stitched to hold each separate colour component, or simply printed on. Printed flags look and are cheap. Obviously if you leave a flag to fly day and night you will shorten its life. Dirty, tatty flags look terrible and should be replaced.

● Shapes

Three shapes are common in sea flags: *rectangular* (which includes *square*, but that is unusual), *swallowtail* and *pennant* (Fig 1).

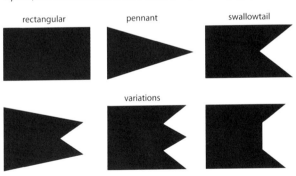

Fig 1 Shapes.

The pennant (or pendant) is triangular, but there are naval and other pennants which are much longer and closer in shape to streamers. The swallowtail is a rectangle with the end cut out. There are variations of this such as a 'sloping' top and bottom so that it is more like a pennant with the end cut. More subtle is a flat inner corner accommodating a stripe (Danish naval ensign). There can also be rare multiple tails, again found in Scandinavia.

WHAT IS A FLAG?

● Parts of a flag

A flag has technical names for its various areas and edges. On a rectangular flag the *dimension* of the long side is called the *length*; the dimension of the short side (against the flag pole) is the *breadth* or the *hoist*. The top edge can also be called the *head*. The bottom edge can be called the bottom or the *foot* (as on a sail). The part flapping in the breeze is the *fly*. A section of the flag to which

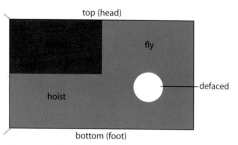

Fig 2 Nomenclature.

reference will frequently be made in this book is the *canton*. This is the upper corner nearest the point of suspension. Usually it consists of a quarter of the flag. *Field* or *ground* describes the background colour of the flag.

Defaced flags

No, this doesn't mean damaged or altered; 'defaced' means a badge, logo or symbol that has been added to an existing design. So a Spanish flag of three simple stripes would be defaced by, for instance, a royal crown or the royal coat of arms. The word 'defaced' usually has a derogatory meaning in English, but in the case of flags it means 'embellished'.

● Proportions

The proportions of a rectangular flag vary, and specific ensigns and national flags have their own exact requirements. British flags have a proportion of 1:2 and this applies to all British-based official flags and ensigns. The Stars and Stripes are a ratio of 50:95. The French *tricolore* and others are in the very different proportion of 2:3.

● Sizes

By tradition, British flag makers' measurements are in yards and multiples of yards, defying most length conventions. European makers will obviously use metric spacing. One leading firm produces its ensigns as half-yard, three-quarters yard, one yard, one-and-a-half, two, etc. Burgees are likely to be supplied in inches, the following rounded numbers being practical: 9 inches, 12, 15, 18, 24, 30, 36, etc (0.23m, 0.30m, 0.38m, 0.45m, 0.60m, 0.76m, 0.91m).

The International Code of Signals flags (see page 47) are in the proportion of 2:3, so a typical size would be 12 x 18 inches (0.30 x 0.45m). Numeral pennants will be twice as long. If code flags are to be read properly then the size of the flag is what matters and not the size of the vessel. However, if they are only used in harbour or for dressing ship and not for 'serious' signalling, then they can be quite small and therefore cheaper. One or two sizable signal flags which describe emergency or urgent situations might be a good compromise. The size given for visibility is 48 inches (1.25m). This is quite big: try code flag standard sizes of 30 inches (0.76m) or 36 inches (0.91m). A usual size for a small yacht is 12 inches (0.30m) by 18 inches (0.45m). When equipping any vessel with flags, the question of the sizes is invariably a problem. Remember that flags look much bigger in your hands than they do aloft.

US and UK yacht clubs conventionally give as a guide for ensigns (in defiance of metrication) one inch (2.54cm) on the fly of the ensign to 12 inches (30cm) of length overall of the vessel. European boats appear to go in for a smaller scale.

American sailors are particularly respectful of the Stars and Stripes and tend to have oversized ensigns, though the flag must not trail in the water. Modern sailing yachts have short overhangs, so the ensign can be larger in proportion to the actual length. This applies to ensign staffs aft. Where the ensign is on a short yard of a power vessel, on the gaff of a mainsail (rare) or on a backstay, then the ensign should be smaller.

The New York Yacht Club recommends to its members that the burgee be approximately half an inch (1.27cm) of fly to each foot (30cm) of the masthead above the waterline on sailing yachts and half an inch for each foot of overall length on powerboats.

House flags, private signals and courtesy ensigns

These flags are smaller. The miniature courtesy flags sometimes seen hoisted, are not very polite to the visited nation and may cause problems in some countries. The house flag or private signal are a rectangular version of the burgee, in respect of size, and can be accorded similar dimensions.

Securing

Flags come with some system for hoisting, usually a line is sewn into the hoist edge. The top corner of this may have a wooden toggle, or the line is lashed or sewn into a loop. At the bottom corner will be the line, say one foot or so, cut off and whipped (Fig 3).

use round turn and two half hitches

use sheet bend

Fig 3 Securing.

To use this for an ensign on a staff, take the halyard with a round turn and two half hitches around the toggle or the loop. A bowline is not suitable as there will be too much length. The line at the bottom is secured to the other end of the halyard with a sheet bend. It can then be hoisted.

An alternative is the Inglefield Clip. This is a simple, secure link and has long been used by professionals to link flags where they are below each other as a signal. The clip would also be on the ends of the halyard. They are very quick to attach and release, very secure when aloft, but less suitable for small boats with only occasional signalling. The yacht burgee is treated quite differently; see below.

All flags when not in use should have dry secure stowage. Larger vessels have dedicated pigeonholes. A yachtsman's alternative is the flag wallet (Fig 4). This is usually used to store the International Code of Signals, but it can be used for other flags. It unrolls to reveal a labelled pocket for each flag, for easy identification.

Fig 4 Flag storage.

Halyards and blocks

A flag hoisted on a staff should not be set too low because of knots and fittings, nor be so tightly hoisted that the bunting (cloth) is forced into the block (Fig 5). A well-designed ensign staff has a sheave and its own cleat on the staff. Hoist it up tight so knots or fittings are hard against the block. Pull the lower part of the halyard tight so that the hoist does not sag away from the staff. On yards, crosstrees or spreaders, sheaves are not suitable. There should be a hanging block, a simple thimble, or an 'eye'. The latter is probably meant for attaching a block, but a light flag halyard can be threaded through it. There is no need for flag halyard blocks to be oversize, they only need to be large enough for the flag halyard.

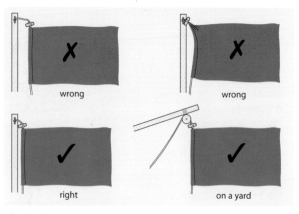

wrong

wrong

right

on a yard

Fig 5 Too loose, too tight.

Shoreside

The usual design for a shoreside flag mast is a vertical mast with a lighter topmast. It also has a yard or gaff projecting from two-thirds of its height: this takes the maritime ensign (which in many cases is also the national flag). Crosstrees are at right angles to the plane of this yard and may well have a number of halyard blocks for flags and signals. The head of the topmast has a block suitable for a burgee or house pennant.

Guarding against vandalism

Vandalism is a potential menace to flags ashore. One method for anti-vandalism is shown in Fig 6).

- The halyard is internal, starting at the bottom with a plate, which can be locked and unlocked, and then travelling up to the sheave at the masthead.

- The lower corner of the flag is attached to a loop with a weight. This loop slides around and up the mast.

- With the upper corner of the flag attached, it is hauled up by access to the lockable plate. The weighted loop keeps the flag in position and taut.

- Once it is hoisted, the halyard is cleated off inside the hollow pole and the access door is locked. There is now no external halyard for anyone to climb or to disturb and this works quite well.

Fig 6 Anti-vandal device.

TYPES OF FLAG

● Ensigns

Some countries, like the UK, have a national flag, *and* a civil or maritime ensign, *and* a naval ensign. The national flag is flown on shore, the civil or maritime ensign is flown by the merchant navy and ordinary yachtsmen, and the naval ensign is reserved for the navy. The maritime ensign therefore is not automatically a replica of the national flag (see page 11). In the UK, for instance, the national flag is the Union flag, and is only flown ashore or on Her Majesty's ships, but the general maritime ensign has the Union flag in the canton and a red field.

Generally, countries with specific ensigns, as opposed to just one national flag, retain their country's identity in the canton but they have different coloured fields. They then have badges or symbols (defacements) for individual or government instititons. Ireland, for instance, an independent republic, has inherited some of the same customs, placing the national flag in the canton, and defacing a blue field for a yacht club ensign (Fig 7).

Fig 7 Ireland – yacht club ensign.

There is a legal requirement for most vessels to have an ensign, and to display it at all the correct times. Rules exist as to where it is worn because its position signifies that the flag in question is indeed an ensign. Flags other than ensigns may not be worn in an ensign position. All leading maritime nations have rules about their own ensigns, however the 191 countries who are signatories to the United Nations Convention on the Law of the Sea (UNCLOS 1982) will be governed by this convention (see Flags and the law, page 59).

Basic UK ensigns

These are white, blue, and red (see Fig 8). That is to say that they have the Union flag in the canton and the fields are white, blue or red. The white ensign showing St George's cross is only flown by ships of the British Navy and members of the Royal Yacht Squadron which is the world's oldest and most senior British yacht club.

Naval ensign (White ensign)

Blue ensign

Civil ensign (Red ensign)

HM Customs and Excise ensign

Fig 8 Some British ensigns.

The (undefaced) blue ensign may be flown on merchant ships where the captain is a member of the naval reserve, on auxiliary naval vessels, on certain government vessels, or used by selected yacht clubs (see Appendix I).

The red ensign (undefaced) is the British merchant ensign and may be, or must be, flown without any special permit on all British ships (see Flags and the law, page 59).

Coastguard ensign

Ships in the service of the Government

Fig 9 More British government ensigns

FORMER UK COLONIES AND THE COMMONWEALTH

There are numerous flags around the world with the British Union flag in the upper canton (Fig 10). This is a legacy of the British empire, but many remain in countries which have since become independent. Yacht clubs in places which were then colonies were granted warrants for blue and defaced ensigns, in exactly the same way as clubs in Great Britain. Some of these yacht clubs have retained their royal warrants and defaced ensigns after independence.

Fig 10 Ensigns of overseas dependencies: Cook Islands and Cayman Islands.

BRITISH GOVERNMENT ENSIGNS

There are 25 blue ensigns defaced by badges, logos, crowns, etc. These may be flown by vessels and shore bases of nominated government departments and officially recognised bodies (Fig 11). There are seven defaced red ensigns of this sort, Trinity House having one of them. There is no special reason why one organisation has blue and another red. These organisations may or may not also fly their own institutional flags, but defaced ensigns obey the normal ensign rules. Yacht clubs are not included in this category.

Fig 11 Ensigns of the Commissioners of Northern Lights and the Commissioners of Irish Lights.

Special ensigns and yacht club special ensigns

There are special ensigns from the UK, Scandinavian countries, the Netherlands and elsewhere. These ensigns are only to be used with permission to the individual person or his appointment/ function.

In the case of the UK there is a confusing array of special ensigns. Various members of specific yacht clubs may fly defaced red, blue or defaced blue ensigns or a white ensign providing they have been granted an Admiralty warrant. (See Appendix for specific yacht clubs.) In the UK this is granted by the Secretary of Defence on behalf of the monarach. There is no correlation between the holding of an Admiralty warrant for a special ensign and having 'royal' in the title of the club. There are 'royal' clubs with and without ensign warrants, there are non-royal clubs with ensign warrants. Whether an ensign is red defaced or blue defaced has no significance.

- Yacht club special ensigns may not be flown unless the respective and corresponding burgee, or flag officer's flag, is flying as well.
- A special ensign applies to a particular owner on a particular yacht. Sailing on a yacht other than his own does not give him the right to fly his special ensign.
- In the UK and its dependencies, misuse of ensigns can attract a considerable fine.

Anguilla

Bermuda

British Virgin Islands

Fig 12 Ensigns of overseas dependencies.

Unlike the special ensigns of government bodies, etc (Fig 9), the yacht club ensign can only be hoisted when the club burgee is flying. The rule is immutable. Therefore unlike the practice with the US ensign (see page 26), the burgee must be hoisted first before the ensign and the ensign lowered prior to the burgee. Other distinct rules surround the use of the yacht club ensign:

- A warrant is granted to an individual yacht and owner in the respective club: only then may the owner fly the special ensign.
- On disposal of that particular yacht, the warrant ceases.
- A warrant cannot be issued for houseboats, etc; the vessel must be genuinely cruising.
- If there are joint owners all must be eligible for the same ensign.

Superiority of ensigns

The unofficial order of superiority for ensigns among yacht clubs is as follows:

- White
- Undefaced blue
- Defaced blue
- Defaced red
- Red

Fig 12a Defaced blue ensign for he Ministry of Defence, Police.

Use on shore

The red ensign can be used on shore, though the general public in Britain would consider it as 'the merchant navy flag'. The white and blue ensigns are maritime flags and their use on shore is usually incorrect. However, there are exceptions. Warranted ensigns may be flown at shore stations of the establishment to which they belong. They must not be flown at the head of a flagpole but should be flown from a yardarm. In an urban setting, a flagpole that comes out obliquely from a building seems acceptable. The white ensign is used at naval establishments. Both may be used for decoration during national festivals (jubilees, war anniversaries etc), if they are 'hung out', suspended on a line or part of a set of small flags.

Courtesy flags

The ensign also has a role as a *courtesy flag*.

- When a vessel is in waters other than those of her own 'ensign country', she shows the maritime ensign of the country being visited.
- If the country has no separate maritime ensign, then she shows a smaller version of the national flag. This is hoisted as soon as she enters foreign territorial waters.
- The courtesy ensign is usually about one third or one half bigger than a signal flag. It should be clean, in good condition and not ridiculously small.
- It is flown from a senior position in the vessel: on a forward mast on ships, from the starboard spreader on yachts. The powerboat equivalent is above any other signals there.
- Yachts engaged in racing do not need to keep the courtesy flag up, but it should be rehoisted after they have crossed the finishing line.

Between some European countries, for instance for yachts in and out of Baltic ports, where a different nation is visited each day, there is some slackness, but it is incorrect not to fly a courtesy flag. EU flags have nothing to do with it and do not affect the rules.

In some countries not flying a courtesy flag is an offence. There are also laws about disrespect to the flag, which include it being torn or dirty. You should check a country's laws on its flags before you arrive (see also Flags and the law, page 59).

Local regional flags are an additional option, but not a substitute. A British boat in a port in Brittany *must* have the French *Tricolore* in the starboard spreaders and she *may care* to hoist the black and white flag of Brittany in an inferior position, ie below the *Tricolore*, or on the port spreader.

FOREIGN YACHTS VISITING OTHER COUNTRIES

Foreign yachts visiting other countries should fly their own ensigns at the rear of their vessels and a small version of their own country's ensign in the starboard spreaders; British yachts should **not** use the British Union flag as a courtesy ensign.

Fig 13 Yachts visting the UK should fly the British red ensign *not* the Union flag.

Ensign of charterer

The custom has arisen for yachts on charter to show an ensign of the charterer's nationality when this nationality is different from the ensign nationality of the vessel. So, a Malaysian owned and registered yacht with an Australian charter party on board will wear the Australian ensign in the rigging and the Malaysian ensign at the ensign staff aft. If she then visits Thailand, she must hoist the Thai courtesy ensign, and not offend her host country. So:

- The Malaysian ensign will be at the stern.
- The Thai ensign at starboard spreader.
- Australian ensign is placed at a position inferior to the Thai courtesy flag, either beneath it or else on the port spreader.

If the charterers are of several nationalities, no more flags should be hoisted and it is probably best to forget the charter ensign!

International ensigns

Examples of nationalities and regions are given below in alphabetical order.

BELGIUM

Belgian ensigns are rectangular, approaching squares (proportion 2:3). The national flag and ensign for vessels in general is the black, yellow and red *Tricolore* (Fig 14). The state ensign has a crown and

Maritime ensign

Yacht ensign (warranted clubs)

Fig 14 Belgium – ensign and yacht ensign.

lion on the yellow. Specified yacht clubs, including the Royal Belgian Yacht Club of Belgium, the Royal Motor Yacht Club of Belgium and the North Sea Yacht Club, with warrants, have a Belgian crown.

DENMARK

Denmark has several ensigns. Most ships show the Danish national white cross on red as the ensign, but the state ensign and naval ensign are the same, only swallow-tailed (Fig 15). A further state ensign has a Danish crown in the top canton of the swallow-tailed flag and is also carried by the royal yacht. The Royal Danish Yacht Club has the swallowtail ensign defaced by the crown, and three stars in the top canton.

State and naval ensign

Fig 15 Denmark.   Yacht ensign

EUROPEAN UNION

The EU (European Union) flag is not an ensign, but it is often seen with French, Dutch, German (see Fig 16), etc national ensigns in the canton. The fly is made up of the EU ring of stars on a blue field. However this flag is not an ensign and has no meaning.

Fig 16 European Union flag with German national colours (no status).

FINLAND

Finland has the same merchant ensign as her national flag. (Fig 17). There is a distinct naval ensign: swallow-tailed and defaced; a state ensign, defaced; a yacht ensign; and a yacht club commodore burgee. The Finnish Åland Islands follow a similar system, but the yacht ensign is swallow-tailed in island colours.

Civil ensign

Naval ensign

Yacht club emblem

Yacht club emblem

Yacht club ensign

Yacht club commodore

Fig 17 Finland.

FRANCE

France has a subtle difference between land and sea for its famous blue, white and red *Tricolore*. On land the stripes are of equal thickness; at sea the thickness from the hoist is 90:99:111; this is said to counteract perspective at a distance. This sea flag is also the jack. The Yacht Club de France has a single white star on the blue of the ensign and a blue star on the white (nothing on the red).

Fig 18 The French ensign and the ensign of the Yacht Club de France.

JAPAN

The national flag and maritime ensign is a red disc on white, but the naval ensign is a smaller red disc with rays from it alternating red and white (Fig 19). This is used by authorised yacht clubs including the Nippon Ocean Racing Club. Other yacht clubs are allocated an undefaced blue ensign with the national flag, plain red sun on white, in the upper canton. The national flag is also the jack. This is similar to the British 'system'.

National flag and maritime ensign

Naval ensign

Alternative yacht ensign

Fig 19 Japanese ensigns.

NETHERLANDS

The tricolour red, white and blue of equal horizontal stripes serves as both national flag and ensign, but there are some defaced special ensigns (Fig 20). The ensign is defaced by crown and fouled anchor for merchant ships commanded by naval reserve officers (cf British blue ensign). Some senior yacht clubs have defaced ensigns, such as the Royal Maas which has its burgee design reappearing in the top canton of the national ensign; and the Royal Netherlands in the centre of the white band. The navy has the national colours in a spiral effect as a jack and there is also a civil jack for optional use which has a slight variation on this design.

Ensign

Royal Netherlands Yacht Club ensign

Fig 20 Netherlands ensigns.

NORWAY

The national flag is also the general ensign (Fig 21). The naval ensign is a triple swallowtail. The customs ensign is the naval ensign defaced in the centre. Selected yacht clubs, including KDY, the Royal Norwegian Yacht Club, have the naval ensign with small defacements in the centre of the cross: the crown with initials, or symbol of the respective club.

Ensign

Ensign of warranted clubs
(defacement varies)

Fig 21 Norwegian ensigns.

REGIONAL FLAGS

Countries with regional areas and identities within them such as Catalonia, Brittany, Lapland, Wales and Scotland have their own flags. However these are not ensigns and should never be flown in ensign positions. They may be offered as courtesy ensigns in the courtesy flag position.

SPAIN

With ensigns for Customs and yacht clubs, Spain also has a jack as well as its national flag and ensign (Fig 22). The Spanish flag and ensign has the royal arms of Spanish union (Castile, Aragon, etc) upon it, but a version without it counts as a civil ensign. Customs has one of these ensigns defaced. Selected yacht clubs are allowed an ensign with a large blue Spanish crown in the centre of the flag. The colours are in the ratio of 5:10:5.

National flag

Fig 22 Spanish ensigns.   Yacht club ensign

UNITED STATES OF AMERICA

The national flag and naval ensign are the same (Fig 23). It commands, and receives, particular respect. There are rules for the flag at sea and ashore. It can fly from a yardarm on shore and be physically below a burgee or special flag, because the yard represents the yard of a ship. It may be at the head of a vertical flag-pole on shore. When on US territory it must be higher, or equal to, others.

TYPES OF FLAG

It is also known as: the Stars and Stripes, Star Spangled Banner or Old Glory. The pattern of stripes dates back to the 17th century (British) East India Company, though the 13 alternate red and white stripes representing the original 13 colonies or states have been in position since 1776. The canton with white stars on blue field started in 1777 with 13 stars: then it grew many times as states were added to the union. The last additional state, number 50, was Hawaii, and that is the number of stars today.

Fig 23 East India Company ensign 1707–1800.

Fig 24 Ensign of USA.

Yacht ensign

Fig 25 USA – flags for non-commercial sailing and power vessels.

Power Squadron flag

Betsy Ross

There is a second ensign for US vessels. This is the yacht ensign (Fig 25), known as the Betsy Ross, which has a fouled anchor in the canton. It is permissible for any recreational craft to wear the yacht ensign. The yacht owner does not have to belong to a club or have a permit to use it. However it is only permissible within the waters of the United States (see Flags and the law, page 59).

On a ship or yacht the US ensign is hoisted at morning colours and lowered at evening colours, or when all the crew leave the vessel. It is hoisted before all other flags and lowered after them. (This differs from some UK yacht clubs.) It is worn from an ensign staff on the stern and the US practice is to show a conspicuously large ensign on any vessel but it is incorrect for the flag to touch the water. Just a reminder here that the US jack (see page 28) is a blue flag with the fifty white stars only and is flown from a jackstaff. There are certain occasions for this and the jack will not be flown on the jackstaff without the Stars and Stripes on the ensign staff. The rules for the Stars and Stripes on land are numerous and do not necessarily apply at sea or on ships. The US ensign is allowed to be flown upside down, but solely as a signal of distress.

Only ensigns are used for dipping (salutes) and half-masted for deaths of national and international figures, owner of the vessel, person in company, club or institution.

● Jacks

This term refers to the small flag worn on a staff at the bows. The position defines the flag so it is not a jack if worn anywhere else. The staff itself is called the jackstaff or even a jack, like the flag.

Like many flag traditions, the jack dates back to the days of sailing warships. A jack was hoisted on the foremost spar (the topmast of the sprit). When these spars were no longer used, the jack was worn on a staff. It was only used in harbour when sails where lowered.

Nowadays a jack is seldom used except on naval ships. British non-naval ships may wear a 'pilot jack' which is the Union flag with a white border, but this is a rare sight. British naval ships wear the Union flag when not under way and not in repair dock. The flag is then called the Union Jack which is the name often given, erroneously, to the British national flag.

Warships of the US wear a blue flag with 50 white stars on a jackstaff. This is the same as the canton of the US national flag. Other nations' navies may fly various jacks: the Dutch are particularly keen on theirs. Occasionally ships and yachts may fly a flag from a jackstaff, but this would be of a trade or house nature and is not a jack merely because it is on the jackstaff.

Fig 26 USA jack.

Fig 27 Dutch civil jack.

The history of the UK Union flag

When James VI of Scotland became King James I of England, he created a new flag to symbolise the united thrones. The English red cross of St George was combined with the Scottish white cross of St Andrew. Later the Union flag became even more complex when the St Patrick's cross of red diagonals on white was added to celebrate the Act of Union with Ireland.

Fig 28 British pilot jack.

- Ships of the British Royal Navy, (and *only* the navy) fly the Union flag as a jack when in harbour or at anchor between colours (sunrise to sunset), or when the ship is dressed overall.
- They will fly it at the masthead (not on the jackstaff) when they have on board the following people:
  - ❏ an Admiral of the Fleet (very few left and a rank which is currently in abeyance);
  - ❏ the First Sea Lord;
  - ❏ former First Sea Lords;
  - ❏ and Admirals who are, or have been, Chief of Defence Staff.
- Naval vessels will fly it at the peak, or on the yardarm, when they are conducting a court martial.
- No other vessel is allowed to fly the Union flag, and it falls under the penalties for carrying improper colours. (See the section on Law)
- British (non-naval) ships may wear a *pilot jack*, which is the Union flag with a white border: It can be worn when dressed overall.

TYPES OF FLAG

● Burgees

The yacht club burgee is the primary flag for most sailing clubs, or associations. The conventional yacht burgee is triangular and usually flown from the head of the main mast. With the proliferation of masthead electronics and other equipment, clubs have been obliged to allow their burgees to be flown at the starboard spreader. This is not entirely satisfactory because other flags may be required at this position and it is often obscured when the sails are hoisted. On dinghies and launches, the burgee may be displayed as a badge on each bow. On a powerboat without any form of mast, the burgee may be worn on a jackstaff on the stemhead. This does not make it a jack and the practice is rare. A few clubs rule that their members may only fly their burgee at the masthead and they forbid other positions.

Burgee facts

- The burgee is a central symbol of the club and will be seen on the masthead of the flagpoles of yacht clubs, whether on a waterfront or in a city. It is also likely to be painted on the front door, printed on stationery, trophies, etc.
- A burgee worn on a sailing yacht indicates that it is not racing. If a yacht is racing, the burgee should not be flying.
- A yachtsman sailing someone else's boat will fly his own club burgee. However, if the owner is in effective control but not actually on board, then his burgee can be worn, eg if the boat is out for a day trip with friends of the owner.

If an owner/skipper is a member of more than one club he may have more than one burgee. Only one can be flown from the masthead. It is incorrect to hoist another burgee on the yacht at the same time. You should fly the burgee belonging to the most local club where the yacht is sailing or of the club running an event in which she is taking part but not actually racing. But there are no hard and fast rules on this and the skipper may show whichever burgee he wishes unless there are club rules which specify otherwise.

Securing a burgee

The yacht club burgee is usually hoisted at the masthead, either on a sailing vessel, powered vessel or on a shoreside mast. There is an exception (see page 68): in order for it to fly clear and be visible, it is usually mounted on a wooden cane (pig stick in the USA) or thin light alloy tube (Fig 29).

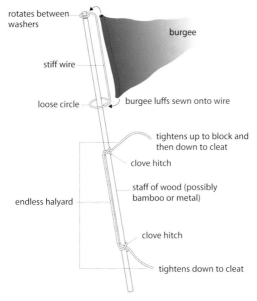

rotates between washers

burgee

stiff wire

loose circle

burgee luffs sewn onto wire

tightens up to block and then down to cleat

clove hitch

staff of wood (possibly bamboo or metal)

endless halyard

clove hitch

tightens down to cleat

Fig 29 How to make a burgee fly true and clear: each burgee needs its own pole.

If the burgee is supplied with a line sewn in and toggle at the head, this should removed. The burgee should then be sewn tightly on to a wire. This wire is then bent to swivel 360° around a pivot at the top and is bent round in a circle so it also swivels around the cane. Each burgee has its own permanent cane.

Flying a burgee

The halyard needs to be endless. Rig a clove hitch six inches or more below the lower end of the swivelling wire. Rig another clove hitch a few inches from the bottom of the cane. The line between the hitches should be taut and lie along the cane. The burgee and cane tend to get tangled in the rigging when you hoist it on a sailing yacht. Take the halyard well out to one side, maintain the tension and hoist it from there. Once the cane is in position at the top, the halyard may be taken back to the base of the mast and made fast to a cleat. Maintain the tension to make the cane stand upright. (Fig 29)

- The sheave at the top of any of these masts is best in the form of a side-mounted block. The cane can lie snug against it and against the surface of the mast.
- If there are masthead instruments, the cane needs to be long enough for the burgee to fly, or droop, clear of the gadgets.
- There is the danger that as you raise the cane or burgee, it may foul these items. For this reason there is a tendency for sailing yachts to hoist the burgee to the spreader. In that case no cane is needed.

The burgee may be flown by day and night when the appropriate person is in charge of the yacht. At night, though, it cannot be seen and its halyard may disturb sleepers. But the awkward job of hoisting and lowering is avoided. At sea it stays up for 24 hours.

Crowns on burgees

Yacht clubs with royal patronage have crowns on their burgees, and/or their ensigns. The British crowns do not necessarily change with each monarch, but they are changed if the new monarch specifically instructs that he/she wants it changed. The current Saint Edward's crown replaced the old imperial crown in 1952 on the instructions of the Queen, when she was crowned, and all yacht club burgees should have been changed at that time.

Flag officers and club officials

The burgees carried by certain club officials differ from the standard burgee of the club. It is a matter for each club's rules whether this is the case, but there is a general usage in Great Britain and those countries which follow its systems. In many countries the president of

Burgee

a yacht club is called the commodore, who may be supported by vice commodore and rear commodore (Fig 31). In Europe, each club has a president and subsidiary officials to that title. Commodores, etc, are described as *flag officers* (even if they never fly a flag, but this follows naval parlance).

Fig 30 Burgee of the Royal Western Yacht Club.

Some clubs appoint an admiral, president, or some distinguished person who ranks above the commodore, but who does not take part in the day-to-day workings of the club. The usual burgee for him or her is the design of the club burgee but on a rectangular flag. Whether one calls this a burgee or a flag is uncertain! All these special burgees follow the same hoisting and flying rules as the club burgee for a member.

There may be further club officials with flags or burgees. One seen occasionally is a 'past commodore' flag either worn at the masthead as a burgee or additional to the club burgee from a spreader; designs for this vary. Occasionally other one-off burgees/flags exist for captains of racing or cruising but these will

Admiral   Commodore

Fig 31 Royal Western Yacht club officers' burgees.

not be found in a reference of standard club burgees and it is likely that only their own club members will know what they mean.

In the UK, the Royal London YC and others allow boats and tenders 'which can conveniently be hoisted on board a yacht' to wear the same special ensign; presumably the burgee would be at the bow. This club unusually allows other club burgees to be flown simultaneously with its own, but only on a second or even third mast. The Royal Western YC specifies that no special ensign should be flown unless the burgee is at the masthead; other clubs have a similar rule (only one club burgee at a time).

Burgee variations

The Royal Canadian Yacht Club follows neither the British nor the US burgee system for flag officers. The committee decided that whilst it would have been logical to emulate the English custom of using balls in the hoist to denote rank, the club already had devices in the hoist. These were (and remain) a crown in the upper hoist and a beaver in the lower hoist. The committee therefore decided to use changes of colour instead. The club burgee is pennant shaped. The patron has the same design in a rectangular flag. The commodore and vice commodore, have swallow-tailed burgees, but in this Canadian system they have small alterations to the ordinary burgee design. The commodore also has an alternative tapering swallowtail.

Fig 32 The members' (left) and Commodore's burgee of the Royal Canadian Yacht Club.

Membership flag

As mentioned, it is nearly always incorrect to show burgees of more than one club at a time. To overcome this some clubs have a membership flag (Fig 34). This is rectangular and usually a slight variation on the club burgee design.

It can be hoisted to a spreader if the burgee of another club is at the masthead. In reality, not many members possess them. Individual club rules may allocate additional special meanings, as set out in respective club rules. For instance, at least one club decrees that if the membership flag is hoisted with its own club burgee aloft, it is said to mean 'members of our club, do come aboard'!

Fig 33 Burgees of the Cruising Association and the Royal Lymington Yacht Club.

Cruising Association
membership flag

Royal Lymington Yacht Club
membership flag

Fig 34 Some clubs and associations have membership flags in addition to regular burgees.

TYPES OF FLAG

United States flag officers

In the US and countries that follow their yachting customs, the system for burgees/flags of club flag officers is totally different from that described above. Instead of a defaced club burgee, there is a uniform system of specific signals to denote flag rank. Four are widely recognised and officially lodged with the Congress of the United States, they are: commodore, vice commodore, rear commodore and fleet captain (Fig 35).

Yacht club commodore

Yacht club vice commodore

Yacht club rear commodore

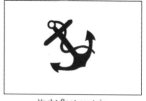

Yacht fleet captain

Fig 35 United States flag officers.

Unlike the British and Canadian flag officers, the eligible yacht owners only fly these flag officer flags at club events and at the club's location. At other times and places the flag officers simply fly the club burgee like any other member. Across the vast waterways of the United States, there are undoubtedly variations and there are some that are rather like the Royal Canadian YC system. They may well also have small stars to designate rank.

Such stars occur in an alternative system currently used by the New York Yacht Club (Fig 36). The higher the rank the more stars they have. This is the reverse of the British system, where the higher the rank the fewer discs on their flags. The club has a standard race committee flag, blue with a red fouled anchor and white letters 'RC'. This is common to many US clubs.

NYYC Burgee

NYYC Commodore

NYYC Vice Commodore

NYYC Rear Commodore

NYYC Past Commodore

NYYC Race Committee

Fig 36 New York Yacht Club flag officers.

TYPES OF FLAG

● Other flags

House flag

This usually means the private signal of a shipping company and is worn at the masthead of a merchant ship. It is sometimes a rectangle, sometimes swallow-tailed. It may be on large freighters or cruise ships, but it can also be seen on local work boats, dredgers, and specialised ships. It may represent the company logo but it is still known as a house flag. There may be a corresponding marking on a funnel. It may also be the personal flag of the owner. There are no rules for design, other than avoiding existing patterns.

It is usually worn by the ship/yacht when in harbour, temporarily in dock, and when the owner is on board. However, commercial shipping lines are inclined to leave theirs flying at sea. It should be flown in an inferior position to any courtesy flags or ensigns (Fig 37).

Cunard

P & O Line

Fig 37 House flags.

Private signal or owner's flag

This is the yachtsman's equivalent to the house flag, but not often seen. Another name for it is the *owner's* flag. It can be any reasonable shape but is usually rectangular or nearly square. In the US the swallowtail shape is traditional. Any design that does not clash with any existing flags is acceptable but initials are not usually used. The flag is worn on a 'subsidiary mast': a second mast on a motor yacht, the foremast of a schooner, or lower down in the rigging. It should not be at the main masthead (though, as stated, this is customary for house flags on commercial shipping), which is reserved for the yacht club burgee. The private signal is not worn by the yacht unless the owner is on board, or effectively based there, visiting a nearby vessel, or ashore locally. Some yacht clubs have a rule which states that when the club burgee is flying, then no private signal may be shown; see the individual club's rules.

H L Brookes   Stanley Woodward Jr

Fig 38 Private signals.

Builder's flag

For commercial craft, warships or yachts, the builder of the vessel may fly his own flag before handing over to the owner. It is a variation of the house flag or private signal. The builder will fly it when the vessel is under way, for instance during sea trials, and until the owner takes possession. Once the owner takes over, the builder's flag should be removed.

Racing flag

The racing flag was similar to a private signal. They are rare these days but can be seen in old photographs on the club wall; and some racing classes may still use them under their own rules.

Previous yacht racing rules demanded that when a yacht was engaged in a race a rectangular or square flag was shown at the sailing yacht's main masthead (Fig 39). It was the same design as the owner's private signal and therefore identified the owner. It also declared that the yacht was racing, thus affecting her conduct on the water. As soon as the boat finished racing, the square flag was lowered and replaced with the burgee. A board with the designs of the flags was displayed on shore during the race.

Once yachts had sails with numbers for identification the racing flag was no longer needed except to indicate the wind angle. With the advent of electronic wind instruments it has become obsolete except on craft without instrumentation. Racing dinghies still occasionally have very lightweight little square flags at their mastheads.

identifiable (owner's racing flag)

minimum size minimum pattern

modern instruments only

Fig 39 Racing flags.

Prize flag

Racing crews hoisted a replica, though possibly a smaller version of the racing flag for each event in the season that had been a first place, so that a 'string' of them was shown for a yacht that had won several times (Fig 40). They were strung on their own flying halyard from the masthead when not under way. For the even more meticulous show-off, flags of similar size with a figure '2' on blue and '3' on red were part of the string to represent second and third prizes. They were flown at the end of a series or season.

Fig 40 Prize flags.

Battle flag

This is a private signal (though never called that) used by racing yachts.

- It is an over-sized flag with a bold design hoisted one third of the way up the forestay of a modern rig when the headsail is not set.
- It is hoisted before or after the actual race, when moving under power, or in harbour. America's Cup boats are often seen flying one when being towed to the starting area of a race.
- It is intended to boost crew morale and a colourful way to intimidate the opposition. (Fig 41).
- The shape varies and there may be twin flags, one above the other, the modern substitute for the old racing and prize flags.

Fig 41 Battle flag with possible second one.

Sponsor flag

If a regatta or race has a commercial sponsor, they may require competitors to fly a flag with the sponsor's design (Fig 42). This should be quite small as flags are a drag and irritation when racing. It is recommended that it is only flown for the minimum time specified and should be removed as soon as the event has ended. The recent practice of flying sponsors' flags from the backstay is quite incorrect and should be avoided.

Fig 42 Sponsor flag.

Association flags

The word 'association' does not represent any one type of yachting institution. If it is in the title of a club-type body with private members, then its flags follow yacht club practice. In the US, classes, racing or production yachts (eg one-designs) may have rectangular or triangular flags. It follows that 'club-type association' burgees cannot be flown with another club burgee, but in the US the class-type association can. In any country which has a national yachting authority, that authority will be a member of the International Sailing Federation (ISAF). If that authority has a flag for use on yachts, this can follow the same procedure as class-type association. However, it is usually only flown at some specific rally or celebration day of the authority itself. In Great Britain there is a rectangular flag available from the national yachting authority: the Royal Yachting Association. However, flying it, except in the circumstances just mentioned, is usually meaningless.

Association of Dunkirk Little Ships

The only vessels, apart from ships with admirals on duty, entitled to fly the St George's flag are members of the Association of Dunkirk Little Ships. They may fly the flag from the jackstaff with their Association flag at the masthead when sailing together in company. Anywhere else afloat it is illegal.

● Defence and official flags

There are hundreds of special flags afloat for various commanders in numerous countries. These are separate from ensigns and are worn from positions in the middle of the ship. Examples are the French *Capitaine de Vaisseau*, and French Customs (Fig 43). Turkish Customs, for instance, has a red flag, but with a white rectangle in its centre enclosing a crescent and star. An Italian police vessel flies a simple red pennant (burgee) with slim yellow fouled anchor.

TYPES OF FLAG

France – Navire des Douanes

France – Capitaine de Vaisseau

Fig 43 French defence flags.

In the United States, combinations of stars and fouled anchors satisfy many requirements. These include naval admirals, marine corps generals, admirals and the Coast Guard.

USA – Admiral

USA – Vice Admiral

Fig 44 US defence flags.

In the UK naval admirals fly the St George's cross (the traditional flag of England, at the masthead; a vice admiral has the same with one disc/ball, rear admiral two discs/balls (Fig 45). These are not ensigns, they are flags of office hence the term 'flag officer'. This is the origin of the British system of yacht club flag officer burgees. When members of the royal family are being conveyed, their launches fly their particular royal standard.

Despite the large number of British maritime organisations, and because of the whole system of ensigns (see page 11) in Great Britain, there are relatively few additional flags for important

Great Britain – Admiral

Great Britain – Vice Admiral

Fig 45 UK defence flags.

government organisations on the sea. However, the ancient Corporation of Trinity House which controls lighthouses and seamarks around England and Wales (Fig 46) has an elaborate flag for its Master and its Deputy Master, and a burgee.

Fig 46 Trinity House ensign and flag.

Fig 47 Cinque Ports flag.

The Commissioners of Northern Lights and the Commissioners of Irish Lights also have pennants and burgees (see page 13). These pennants are flown from tenders, working vessels and shore stations. Other notable British flags afloat are those of the Royal National Lifeboat Institution, which also functions throughout Ireland. One complicated but ancient flag is that of the Lord Warden of the Cinque Ports (Fig 47). These five harbours in south-east England were designated specific privileges and duties in the 12th century. Some of these ports have silted up and are no longer accessible by sea and the title has become historic.

Code flags

The International Code of Signals (described in detail in the following section) is a set of flags each with a specific meaning. Each sender or recipient can decode the flags in his own language, and arrive at the equivalent text, so this system crosses all language barriers.

INTERNATIONAL CODE OF SIGNALS

They are a distinctive set of coloured flags. There are 26 letters and 10 numerals (0 to 9), three *substitutes* (UK) or *repeaters* (US) and one *answering pennant*. They are rarely used to spell out words, but they are valuable for coded messages. They can then be decoded in the official book of the International Code of Signals. Sailors should familiarise themselves with some of the more important ones.

Semaphore

One system for communication by flags was *semaphore* (Fig 48). Semaphore is now obsolete. Each letter of the alphabet and each numeral, had a unique position for one or both flags. Words were spelt out letter by letter to an observer. However it was a laborious system and has been superceded by the International Code of Signals and modern communications.

Fig 48 Semaphore.

CODE OF SIGNALS

 ANSWERING PENNANT

A – Alpha

I have a diver down: keep well clear at slow speed

B – Bravo

I am taking in, or discharging or carrying dangerous goods

C – Charlie

Yes, affirmative

D – Delta

Keep clear of me: I am manoeuvring with difficulty

E – Echo

I am altering my course to starboard

F – Foxtrot

I am disabled: communicate with me

G – Golf

I require a pilot.
By fishing vessels I am hauling in nets

H – Hotel

I have a pilot on board

I – India

I am altering my course to port

J – Juliet

I am on fire and have dangerous cargo: keep well clear of me

K – Kilo

I wish to communicate with you

L – Lima

You should stop your vessel instantly

M – Mike

My vessel is stopped and making no way through the water

N – November

No, negative

O – Oscar

Man overboard

P – Papa

Vessel about to put to sea
By fishing vessels My nets are caught fast

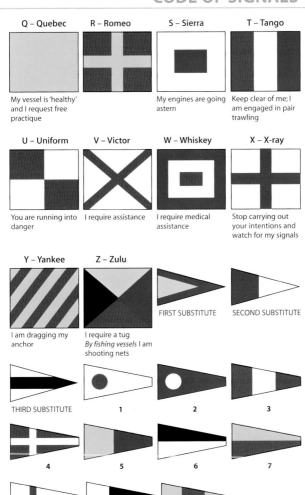

Q – Quebec

My vessel is 'healthy' and I request free practique

R – Romeo

S – Sierra

My engines are going astern

T – Tango

Keep clear of me; I am engaged in pair trawling

U – Uniform

You are running into danger

V – Victor

I require assistance

W – Whiskey

I require medical assistance

X – X-ray

Stop carrying out your intentions and watch for my signals

Y – Yankee

I am dragging my anchor

Z – Zulu

I require a tug
By fishing vessels I am shooting nets

FIRST SUBSTITUTE

SECOND SUBSTITUTE

THIRD SUBSTITUTE

1

2

3

4

5

6

7

8

9

0

The flags must be visible, identifiable, and not too small even if the vessel is small. Some very small flags are sold in yacht chandlers. These are impracticable for passing any kind of message and are mostly sold for decoration (see Dressing ship, pages 73–5)

There are two-, three- and four-flag messages. These can be found in the International Code of Signals, published by the International Maritime Organisation (IMO). There are also three Tables of Complements, each of which provides for specific situations such as towing, medical problems, times, dates, positions and bearings, etc. When added to the main code signals they expand the vocabulary to several thousand messages.

In the US there is also an extra flag for 'I have a diver down, please keep clear'. This is a red flag with a diagonal white stripe. The code flag T is used in the United States to request a launch service.

Code messages are never more than four flags which is why there are only three substitutes. If there is a series of messages, then the group of flags is hoisted until it has been observed, then another different combination is sent up. In theory (though it is hardly, if ever, used today) there is an order for reading flags by using different positions in the rigging. This is:

- Masthead
- Triatic stay
- Starboard yardarm
- Port yardarm

It is possible that a modern yacht might want two signals at once. If that is the case then the starboard yardarm (or spreader) is always read before the port one.

The three substitute or repeater pennants are available so that a letter or number can be repeated, even though the ship has only a single set of the code. The first substitute repeats the first flag of a group; the second substitute repeats the second; the third repeats the third. So the number 2277 would show as: numeral 2, first sub, numeral 7, third sub (because the first 7 was the third flag in the group). The answering pennant is used to acknowledge a signal, as a decimal point among figures, and for naval ships to indicate that they are using the International Code of Signals and not the naval code of signals.

● Yacht only signal flags

In the US there are long-established conventional yacht signals, that cannot be described as private; yet they do not apply to commercial, or working vessels. Abroad, for instance, in a Caribbean anchorage where there are yachts from a number of nations, other American skippers would probably understand them. They can also be used by foreign yachts in the USA (Fig 49).

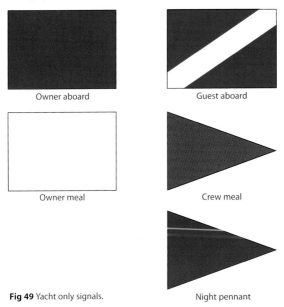

Owner aboard

Guest aboard

Owner meal

Crew meal

Fig 49 Yacht only signals.

Night pennant

CODE OF SIGNALS

These include:

- *Owner absent flag* – the owner is temporarily absent will be back eventually.
- *Guest aboard flag* – there is a guest on board but not the owner.
- *Owner meal flag* – owner eating and visitors not welcome.

These last two signals, though long established are now known as optional, while the simple owner absent flag is still recommended.

● Naval codes

Navies have their own code flags for signalling. It is not necessary for civilians to be able to read these signals. However, if a naval ship is flying the answering pennant of the International Code, it means that she is using the International Code and expects to be understood by merchant captains and yachtsmen. Yacht racing occasionally makes use of the naval numerals in addition to the International Code numerals. Naval code numerals are rectangular and not pennant shaped (Fig 50). This naval code is standardised for NATO and so applies in the United States, Canada and European member countries of NATO.

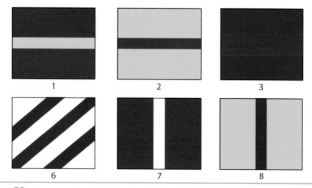

1	2	3
6	7	8

● Flags used for signalling distress

Electronic communication has immensely improved systems for rescuing people in distress at sea, but there are still flag signals that request help. The definition of distress should be understood. *Distress* is where a boat or person is in imminent danger and requires immediate assistance. Any distress communication has priority over all other messages. *Urgency* is a lesser degree, concerning safety of a boat or a person; for instance a vessel disabled but not sinking, or a medical matter. *Safety* is the third grade and is essentially an alert, for example a navigational or meteorological warning. The flag signals for distress (Fig 51) are:

- ■ The International Code flags NC hoisted one above the other
- ■ Any square flag, any colour, with a ball above or below it

Three single letter signals of Urgency which apply here are:

- ■ **V** I require assistance
- ■ **W** I require medical assistance and safety
- ■ **U** You are running into danger

Fig 50 Naval numerals.

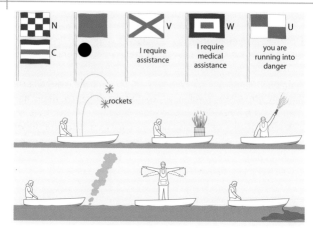

Fig 51 Some visual distress and safety signals at sea.

Visual distress signals

Other visual signals for distress are:

- Flashing Morse SOS by light, red parachute or hand-held flares
- Orange smoke
- Repeated slow raising and lowering of arms on each side of the body
- Flames on the vessel (as from a burning oil barrel)
- Orange dye marker in the water
- A piece of orange canvas marked with a black square and circle or appropriate symbol.

The last two are for recognition from the air.

● Racing code flags

The International Code and other flags have specific meanings in yacht and sailing dinghy racing and are used in conjunction with guns and hooters.

Competitors need to know them and a general knowledge of them by other vessels will avoid conflict on the water. Races are started and finished from a committee boat, a shore station, or a platform of some sort. The start and finish may not necessarily be in the same place. The finish of an ocean race may be thousands of miles from the start.

Yachts engaged in racing fly:

- Class flags (code flags or numeral pennants or a distinctive house flag) off their backstays
- No burgee
- No ensign after the five minute gun

So if you approach a fleet of yachts flying numeral pennants, code flags, or distinctive identical flags and no ensigns and no burgees, it is a fairly safe bet that they are racing and are best avoided. Racing boats will be sailing around tactically while these signals are in use. Look for each end of the starting line, marked by buoys or the committee boat. The committee boat and auxiliary boats running the event may fly a variety of flags. There may be more than one class starting, so a series of starting signals might be on the move: up and down flag halyards. Flags used in controlling races are in Fig 52 and include the answering pennant and substitutes.

CODE OF SIGNALS

Postponement signals

Postponement

Races not started
are postponed

Postponement and no
more racing today

Signals before the start

Class flag

5 minutes to start

4 minutes to start
or flag 1 and/or flag Z
or Black flag

Class flag

1 minute to start
Preparatory flag removed

Starting penalties

Round-an-end rule is
in effect

Soft penalty (20%) rule is
in effect

Black flag rule is in effect

Course change signals

Shorten course

Position of next race
mark changed

Other signals

Collect new instruction or
follow this boat

Fig 52 Flags in yacht and dinghy racing ISAF signals.

Abandoment signals

1 hour delay

Postponement of 1–6 hours are indicated by the appropriate numeral pennant

Abandonment
When flown above code flag A or H, indicates that there will be no more racing today

Start and finishing line

Class flag

Start

Start line

Finishing line

Recall signals

Individual recall

All yachts recalled

Protest signals

Time limit for protests is in effect

Mark replacement

Lifejackets must be worn

Boat taking a scoring penalty

FLAG ETIQUETTE

There are quite a few reasons for flying flags:

- *Recognition, and a legal requirement* An ensign declares the origin of the vessel, probably indicates the common language on board, and is usually a legal requirement.
- *Authentication* Particular flags represent the river police, Customs, or a local authority.
- *Information and communication* The International Code of Signals is designed to impart meanings that will be understood by all who recognise flags across several languages.
- *Political gestures* Welcoming a head of state (or flag burning).
- *Decoration* Decoration for celebration: yachts *dressed overall* will have crews in a festive mood and it's party time.

● Flying the minimum

The minimal flag display on a vessel depends on the duties or nature of the ship. The obvious minimum is simply the maritime ensign which is a flag flown on a vessel to show its nationality. This applies to all nations. In general, captains and owners are proud to show their nationality. This particularly applies if they are abroad. A working boat at home, such as a dredger, however, is more likely to display signals indicating its function and wear no ensign. Any vessel working in a foreign country should hoist its national ensign. It indicates a possible language difference and the vessel's legal position. Fishing boats are exempt from displaying ensigns.

It used to be common for a yacht in home waters to wear only the yacht club burgee at the masthead. Today it is more likely that there will be no burgee, but there will be an ensign.

Q Flag and courtesy flag

Vessels visiting a foreign country *and requiring customs clearance* should display the yellow Q flag as well as the courtesy flags discussed on pages 16–17. The Q flag declares 'my vessel is healthy and I request free pratique'. In other words the yacht requires customs clearance so that the crew can come ashore. Yachts from European Union member states travelling within the EU will not require customs clearance and therefore have no need to fly the Q flag (See International Code of Signals page 48).

● Flags and the law

Legal requirements concerning flags are most likely to apply to the ensign and other national flags. Each country has its own laws. Misuse of flags can invoke fines. In the USA the national flag, which is also the merchant and naval ensign, is still controlled under Acts of Congress. A fairly recent debate was for 'the flag desecration constitutional amendment' which would have made burning the US flag a punishable crime. It was defeated in the Senate.

Merchant Shipping Act

British yachts are treated as merchant vessels and therefore have to comply with the Merchant Shipping Act which was amended in 1995. Certain ensigns afloat were regulated by the Merchant Shipping Act of 1894. The 1995 Act applies to Great Britain, Northern Ireland and certain British overseas dependencies. In brief it states that: Any British ship/yacht is *entitled* to fly an undefaced red ensign. British registered ships/yachts, (either under Part 1 of the Merchant Shipping Act, or on the Small Ships Register) are *required* to fly an undefaced red ensign (see page 11). Vessels are classed as a 'small ship' if they are under 24m (79ft) long. Equally correct are alternative ensigns whose owners have the relevant Admiralty warrants to fly them (see Ensigns page 13), and an assortment of government ensigns (see Appendix 1).

FLAG ETIQUETTE

In the case of British territories, ships registered in a particular territory may fly the appropriate defaced or modified ensign. The same Act states when the lawful ensign shall be hoisted by a British ship 'other than a fishing vessel'.

When does a British ship/yacht hoist her lawful ensign?

- On entering or leaving any foreign port.
- For ships of 50 or more gross tons: on entering or leaving any British port.
- On a signal being made by one of Her Majesty's ships, including any ship under the command of a commissioned naval officer. (See page 52 for signals.)

Individual nations also have their own specific laws regarding their flags and yachtsmen are advised to make themselves aware of them before arriving in that country. Local bye-laws often exist on rivers and in harbours, and yachtsmen have a duty to establish what they are and to comply with them.

The Law of the Sea

It is impractical to review the laws of every maritime country, however the United Nations Convention on the Law of the Sea (UNCLOS) was adopted in 1982 and signed by 191 countries. It superseded the Geneva Convention of 1958. Vessels belonging to countries which are signatories to the Convention are bound to comply with the Law of the Sea. They also usually have an obligation under their national laws to show their nationality when it is required. Failing to do so can leave the vessel open to being boarded and impounded.

Penalties associated with flag flying

There are penalties for British ships flying the alternative special ensigns without the required warrants, and certain other flags. The other flags which attract penalties include any flags and pennants worn by Her Majesty's ships, and the Union Flag (erroneously known as the Union Jack).

Officials may board the offending vessel, seize the flag and arrange prosecution of the owner or master. The penalty varies but is currently a substantial fine. So a yachtsman who has the cheek to fly a white ensign for instance without holding a warrant for it, would fall foul of this law. Foreign registered yachts using the Union Flag as a courtesy flag in the UK would be incorrect but they would probably be exempt from prosecution under this Act because they are not British ships. Deliberately failing to fly a national flag when it is required, outside or within the UK, can incur a fine of up to £50,000. The officials who may enforce this law are: a commissioned naval or military officer, a Customs and Excise officer, or a British consul.

It is also an offence for a foreign registered vessel to impersonate a British vessel by flying a British ensign unless she is attempting to escape capture by an enemy. Why it is thought that a British ensign might save a foreign vessel from attack remains a mystery. These days, in certain parts of the world, it is thought that British and American ensigns might actually have the reverse effect, and invite attack!

● Hoisting times

Since flags cannot be seen at night, there is no point in having them aloft after dark. Occasionally on land, and sometimes on a vessel in harbour on certain occasions, a flag may be illuminated. The royal standard on Windsor Castle, for instance, is hoisted and floodlit during the hours of darkness.

FLAG ETIQUETTE

Hoisting times for ensigns

- In British water, in harbour or at anchor, the British ensign is hoisted (or made) at 0800 local summer time.
- In European waters the hoisting time is 0900 between 1 November and 14 February.
- In American and tropical waters the seasons are less defined and the hoisting time is 0800 all year.
- In far northern and southern winters, when sunrise is after 0900, the ensign is hoisted at sunrise or follows local custom.

Naval ships and ships with 'ceremonial crews' (for example, training ships) may hoist all necessary flags simultaneously. Yachts and working boats should hoist the ensign first and then work through the other signals, if any. In the case of yachts with British and Commonwealth special ensigns (see page 14), the yacht club burgee must be hoisted before the ensign. In theory, the actual time of hoisting and lowering is taken from any warship present, the yacht club on shore, or the senior (yacht club) officer present.

● Lowering

Lowering (or *striking*) ensigns and other flags is traditionally at sunset around the world. However in high latitudes in the summer, where it may be light almost all night, an arbitrary time can be chosen, usually 2100 local time. If all members of a yacht's crew go ashore before sunset the ensign should be lowered before they leave so that it will not be left flying after sunset, which is not good form. Shore stations and yacht clubs follow the same procedures with ensigns – as if they were a ship moored near that position.

Racing

Ensigns are struck (lowered) at the five minute gun. When the race is over, or the yacht has retired, she raises it again to indicate that she is no longer bound by racing rules.

Timings for burgees and other flags

Customs vary about the timings for flying yacht club burgees, house flags and courtesy flags. The general practice today is for these to be left flying for as long as they are required. So the burgee simply stays up until the owner departs, or for other valid reasons. Some yacht clubs may have rules which require the burgee to follow the same timings as the ensign.

Sometimes the rules state that 'colours shall be hoisted'. (*Colours* is a naval term meaning any flag which displays nationality, usually the ensign or jack.) The best advice is:

- Leave the burgee aloft.
- Lower the ensign for the night.
- The courtesy flag can stay hoisted, which might save problems with a policeman having an early stroll down the dock!

These rules apply in harbour, alongside, on a mooring, anchored in a bay or anywhere else; or even temporarily hauled out ashore.

At sea

Once out at sea the ensign should be struck. There is no one else to see it and it suffers heavy wear with the apparent wind on the vessel. On a small yacht or working boat, the whole ensign staff may be removed for safety.

British yachtsmen are not legally required to fly an ensign at sea unless they are signalled to do so by one of Her Majesty's ships (see Law), or by a ship under the command of a commissioned naval officer. This signal is likely to be Code VF ('You should hoist your identity signal') or CS ('What is the name or identity signal of your vessel or station?') If the navy wants you to declare your identity by hoisting your ensign then it is not a bad idea to go along with the request before they use you for target practice!

The burgee stays aloft; but the courtesy flag, if any, is lowered.

Approaching a foreign harbour

During the hours when ensigns are hoisted, all vessels should re-hoist their ensign on approach to a foreign harbour in order to show their nationality as required under international law. Courtesy and Q flags should also be flown if required. At sea it makes sense to hoist the national colours (the ensign) if passing close to another vessel.

In the US, New York Yacht Club rules state that if a yacht enters or leaves port outside the times for hoisting and lowering, but there is enough daylight to sight the flags, then the yacht should show her ensign. It should be lowered once the yacht has moored or reached open sea. This rule seems a common sense recommendation for others, even if not strictly in accordance with all written rulings.

● Positions of ensigns

In the days of sailing warships, each position from which a flag was flown, had distinct significance, apart from the image of the flag itself. The positions from which flags are flown today are handed down from that time, with modifications. These may vary between sea and harbour.

Commercial ships still have some form of mast, though these have diminished since the days of sail. Even so, it will usually have facilities to hoist the ensign on an aft facing spar of some sort and signal flags either side. The merchant or other ensign is the most important 'permanent' flag. In harbour (anchorages, rivers etc) on all types of vessel, it is flown from an ensign staff at the stern (Fig 53a). This staff slants aft and is on the centreline unless there is gear that makes this impossible, in which case it should be mounted on the starboard quarter. So at sea on most types of vessel the ensign will be flown on the aft staff or from a spar on the main mast, such as from the end of the gaff boom. Once in harbour the ensign should be moved to the aft staff.

Fig 53a Position of ensign on staff at the stern.

Fig 53b Position of ensign on gaff rig.

Fig 53c Position of ensign on leech of sail.

Fig 53d Position of ensign on two-masted vessel.

Other ensign positions

Back in the days of sailing ships, the ensign at sea was flown from the gaff of the mizzen. It is still correct on a gaff-rigged yacht to hoist the ensign at the end of the gaff of the aftermost mast (Fig 53a). It does mean, though, that you will have a halyard wrapped across the sail which will require adjustment with the sail (Fig 53c). When the sail is lowered, the ensign will have to be transferred to the aft staff.

Fig 54a Position of ensign on backstay.

Fig 54b Position of ensign on yard or gaff.

Another permissible position for a two-masted vessel (ketch, yawl or schooner) is at the head of the aft most mast (Fig 53d).

Modern sailing yachts sometimes hoist the ensign on the backstay because this is near the position of the conventional ensign staff (Fig 54a). This applies especially to racing yachts which try to save weight. It is reasonable, but not very elegant.

Ensigns on powerboats

- On powerboats the ensign can be on the same stern ensign staff at all times.
- At sea it can be flown on a yard or gaff specially rigged on the mast for this purpose (Fig 54b).
- Once the motorboat or yacht has entered harbour, the ensign must be transferred to the aft staff. However it does look smart on a yard and this is particularly common on official small craft such as Customs' and harbour masters' launches.
- It may be that a separate ensign will have to be used for each position because the ensign on the yard is usually smaller than the ensign on the aft staff owing to lack of space.

Seniority of positions

For all vessels it is assumed that there is at least one mast and that this has crosstrees or spreaders). The ensign is never hoisted on the single mast except on a yard. The masthead is reserved for the house flag (for commercial shipping) or the yacht club burgee. It is never used for signals. Thereafter the *seniority* of positions is:

1 Starboard spreader, hoisted close up.
2 Port spreader hoisted close up.
3 Below top flag on the starboard spreader or on starboard inner halyard.
4 Below top flag on port spreader, or on port inner halyard.

Other places where flags may be flown

- On a second mast, ie foremasts or mizzens
- On a jackstaff in the bows

If you have to place flags below each other on the same halyard, use spans for clarity and try not to offend 'important' flags (see Fig 55).

Fig 55 Positions and seniority of other flags.

FLAG ETIQUETTE

What goes where?

Problems arise when more than one signal is desired. If there are only two or three completely different flags, then it is quite simple. A sailing yacht may have: an ensign at the stern; a burgee at the masthead (or main masthead); a courtesy ensign at the starboard spreader, if applicable, or another signal, such as a flag of the International Code. However, the situation may not be that easy. Today masthead electronics and other equipment make it difficult to find room for the club burgee so it has to be moved to the starboard spreader.

If a courtesy ensign is needed, it would be discourteous to the country you are visiting to fly it below your club burgee. In this case, the courtesy ensign must be close up to the starboard spreader and the burgee transferred to port. If there is a signal (for instance the Q flag requesting Customs clearance) it can go below the burgee to port (Fig 56).

Fig 56 Position of flags on starboard and port spreader (left) and position of flags on motor cruiser mast (right).

The ideal arrangement is to have the burgee at the masthead, the courtesy flag at the starboard spreader and the international signal flag close up to port. Flying the burgee at the masthead does create space when further flags are needed. Techniques for coping with this are looked at on page 30. The same system is used on a motor cruiser provided that she has a suitably rigged mast. (Fig 56). If she does not have this, then the flags should be displayed as near as possible to match this pattern.

Certain yacht clubs do not allow their burgee to be hoisted at the spreader or crosstrees: these include the Royal Yacht Squadron and Royal Cruising Club, whose rules insist that you use the masthead.

● Positions of other flags

A house flag (see page 38) or private signal, should be at the starboard spreader (or port spreader if a burgee is already there). In vessels with two masts (sail or power), it should be flown from the head of the shorter mast (not the main mast). It should not be flown at sea, and is usually flown only when the owner is on board. On a motorboat it should go on the stubmast if one is available; failing that it will have to go on the jackstaff.

Burgee on a mastless vessel

If there is no mast: the burgee can be flown from the jackstaff in the bows (Fig 57).

Fig 57 Flags on staff in bows of craft with no mast.

All other flags

Other flags, such as the US guest flags and meal flag, are located in decreasing seniority of positions, starting with starboard spreader, outer halyard as above.

The jackstaff is primarily for what it says, the *jack*. It may, however, carry the burgee on a mastless vessel, and possibly the owner's house flag or 'private signal'. Certain countries have a national jack hoisted there under strict regulations at certain times. Commercial vessels usually have a jackstaff, as do many motor yachts if they have a socket welded on the pulpit. Sailing vessels seldom have a permanent arrangement owing to the requirements of the rig.

Maritime flags ashore

Land flags are not permitted at sea except under particular circumstances, but maritime flags are allowed on shore as long as the establishment is reasonably near the water and that they are hoisted correctly. The exceptions to the 'near water' rule are:

- Naval establishments well inland
- Nautical establishments inland (schools for ships' officers, headquarters of pilotage or Customs)
- Recognised yacht clubs in city locations

SHORE MASTS

These consist of a main mast; possibly with a topmast; a cross yard or crosstrees; or a yard or gaff. The yacht club burgee or permitted official signal flies from the top of the vertical mast. Halyards run down from the crosstrees for any required signals (including 'reverse' courtesy ensign for visiting foreign nationals). The appropriate ensign (naval, national, merchant, yacht, or special ensign) flies from the yardarm and not from the masthead (Fig 58).

Fig 58 Flags on shore mast.

● Salutes

As is widely known, but not much practised, flags are used at sea for salutes. It is an international usage and it is the ensign that is used for this; never the burgee or other flags. It is not obligatory but a traditional courtesy. The procedure is to *dip the ensign* as follows:

- The saluting vessel lowers the ensign about two-thirds of the way down the ensign staff (3).
- It stays there (*at the dip*) while the vessel being saluted does the same (4).
- After a pause, she then re-hoists hers fully (5).
- As soon as this is observed the saluting vessel (6) also re-hoists her ensign (Fig 59).

Fig 59 Saluting.

Whom do you salute?

- Salute royal yachts, warships of all nationalities and possibly flagships of great shipping lines (though response is doubtful);
- Flag officers of your own yacht club, but only on first meeting.
- Some shoreside yacht clubs (with shore masts) may be saluted once as yachts sail past. 'Once' varies with the club: it might be at the beginning of the season, at the beginning of a regatta, or some other occasion.
- Warships never dip their ensigns to anyone in salute, only in acknowledgement.

Vessels which take salutes, take them whether under way, at anchor or moored. The ensign must only be dipped by lowering the halyard as described; not, for instance by holding the staff and waving it up and down! A yacht club vessel, on race committee duties, neither dips nor acknowledges any salutes.

● Mourning

There is public and private mourning with flags. These consist of hoisting the ensign only at half-mast. There is one exception: see death of the yacht's owner page 73. Strictly speaking the ensign is hoisted to the mast or staff head and then lowered so that it is about one third (not actually half) of the way down the halyard. Note that this is a different position from a *dip salute*. Again, the correct form at sunset is to hoist the ensign fully, pause for a few seconds and then lower completely.

There are also restrictions on *half-masting* the US ensign. Do not half-mast the burgee unless the owner has died.

All vessels in port (half-masting does not apply at sea) should follow local practice. The matter may be for a local or national dignitary. In some countries there are half-mast days for observing a historical event.

Fig 60 Mourning.

When do you half-mast?

On news of the death, for a number of days afterwards and on the day of the funeral. Yacht or ship owners may wish to mark the passing of someone known personally to them and again the ensign is half-masted (Fig 60).

On Memorial Day, USA (last Monday in May), ensigns are half-masted from 0800 to 1220. A twenty one gun salute starts at 1200 hours and lasts twenty minutes, hence the finish at 1220.

Death of the owner

The death of the owner of the yacht is marked by half-masting both the ensign *and* the burgee. On the first sunset, all are lowered for the last time. The Royal Yacht Squadron states that it should be until sunset on the day of the funeral; the New York Yacht Club, contrary to remarks above, half-masts the burgee (and private signal), but *not* the ensign on the death of a member of the club. Other clubs and nations may have variations. If a salute (dip) has to be made, then the ensign is first hoisted to full height before proceeding.

● Dressing ship

This is a 'flag fiesta' when most code flags are hung out to dry. Sometimes yachts dress overall for a club regatta day – take your lead from the club and flag officers. Vessels often dress overall at their launching or commissioning or when there is to be a ceremony. If, while on a vessel in a foreign port, you find there is an official festival, join in by dressing your yacht.

The recommended order from forward for code flags is: E, Q, p3, G, p8, Z, p4, W, p6, P, p1, I, answering pennant, T, Y, B, X, 1st substitute, H, 3rd substitute, D, F, 2nd substitute, U, A, O, M, R, p2, J, p0, N, p9, K, p7, V, p5, L, C, S. It is suggested that the line up to the masthead ends at '3rd substitute' and starts again towards aft at 'D'.

In the US the order is different and, starting from forward, is as follows: AB2, UJ1, KE3, GH6, IV5, FL4, DM7, PO Third substitute/ Repeater, RN First Repeater, ST Zero, CX9, WQ8, ZY Second Repeater.

Dates for dressing ship

In the UK the official dates of celebration and for dressing ship are:

- Accession Day, 6 February,
- Commonwealth Day, the second Monday in March
- HM The Queen's real birthday, 21 April
- Coronation Day, 2 June
- HM The Queen's Official birthday: (the date is published annually by signal from the Yeoman of the Admiralty)
- HRH The Duke Of Edinburgh's birthday, 10 June.

Fig 61 Dressed overall.

In the US two days for dressing overall are: Independence Day, 4 July, and President's Day, the third Monday in February. In France it is Bastille Day, 14 July, and in other countries it is likely to be on days of national celebration.

How to dress

Flags are flown from the stemhead of the vessel, to a masthead, to any other masthead(s), then down to the after end of the vessel (see page 74). On gaff rigs, which have not got single backstays, a topsail halyard or a topping lift is used to run flags to the end of the boom and one or two further flags are suspended from the boom and bowsprit ends. The flags used are those of the International Code of Signals plus any other code (eg naval numerals). Certain other flags may be seen in specific positions, as mentioned below, but in the general sequence *no* ensigns, *no* private signals, *no* burgees, *no* inflated fish, streamers or skull and crossbones!

The code sequence for the flags is intended to ensure that no signal is made inadvertently and that the colours are pleasantly contrasting. The order is listed overleaf. For etiquette sticklers, there are specific places for ensigns and burgees.

UK waters

For national days in UK waters, the ensign shall be flown from the masthead and other mastheads. The burgee should also be on the main masthead (so it will be a mess!). If the person on board is a club flag officer, the flag officer's burgee is flown and no ensign on the main mast. If there is only one mast (as is likely), then no ensign is hoisted to the masthead. The jackstaff carries the correct national jack (British Union flag with a white border).

For local occasions, launchings, regattas, etc, no ensign is shown at the main masthead – just the usual burgee – but the ensign may be hoisted on other masthead(s), if any. In all cases, where there are 'multiple' masts a special ensign may be on one (or on the ensign staff aft) and red ensigns on the others. In all these cases the correct jack (see page 29) may be hoisted on the jackstaff.

FLAG ETIQUETTE

International waters

Elsewhere for festivals, the courtesy ensign is hoisted at the 'non-main' masthead, ie foremast or mizzen masthead. The UK ensign is worn at the other mastheads. If there is one mast, it carries the foreign ensign plus club burgee (but again to be correct a flag officer flies his burgee and not the (foreign) ensign. We think that, although what is just stated is correct, it would be more courteous to ignore it. In other words, hoist the foreign ensign to the masthead and the flag officer's burgee at the spreader (if, apparently, it is not to be besmirched by an ensign!).

Shore stations

Maritime shore establishments and yacht clubs, provided they have a mast as described earlier with topmast, crosstrees and yard, shall hoist International Code flags in the same way as a ship or yacht. The run of flags can be from near the ground up via the crosstree, across to the mast and down the other side. No ensign is hoisted to the masthead; it remains hoisted on the yard.

Dressing ship is for harbour or anchorage use only. Once the vessel is under way, the code flags should be lowered. However the ensigns remain at the respective mastheads. Ensigns used for dressing ship are not dipped in salute.

Fig 62 Dressed under way.

● Getting it right

Paint it on?

High speed craft such as racing powerboats cannot carry flags in the conventional manner. Painting an ensign or burgee on the hull or super-structure is acceptable but for British vessels it is the ensign which should be painted on and not the Union flag. It is traditional to have a yacht club burgee on a plaque on either bow of a yacht's launch or dinghy.

Burgee rights and wrongs

Yacht club burgees around the world may frequently be unrecognised, but that is no reason for not using them. Generally speaking the view is that a small triangular flag at the masthead or at the starboard spreader should only be a yacht club burgee.

- Don't fly the burgees of more than one club at a time.
- Don't fly burgees or flags that you find in a drawer of the charter yacht if you don't know what they are. They might not be burgees; they might belong to flag officers of a club.

✗ WRONG

✗ NO STATUS

✗ ILLEGAL

unknown regional flag

European Union flag with national colours

Flag of St George

Fig 63 Non-ensigns. Regional and sub-national land flags are not ensigns.

- Do fly your own club burgee on a yacht you have chartered if you want to.
- Do fly your club burgee with its appropriate ensign.
- Do fly club membership flags with another burgee if you like.

FLAG ETIQUETTE

Don't

✗ Don't leave large promotional flags flying. They can be very noisy and irritate others who want to spend a quiet afternoon on their boats.

✗ Don't buy cheap printed flags.

✗ Don't fly St George's crosses, Union flags or any other land flags from a yacht.

✗ Don't buy courtesy flags that are offensively small.

✗ Don't offend a senior flag by flying something else above it.

✗ Don't offend a courtesy flag when visiting a foreign country.

✗ Don't fly anything except ensigns or racing flags from the ensign position.

Do

✔ Lower any flags when you leave the vessel.

✔ Keep them clean and in good repair.

✔ Fly flags that are a reasonable size.

✔ Fly them in the correct positions.

✔ Take them down when not required.

✔ Buy sewn flags and not printed ones.

✔ Make sure you know what is expected when you visit another country.

INTERNATIONAL YACHT CLUB BURGEES

Pairs of selected yacht club burgees and ensigns in alphabetical order.

Cruising Association

Cruising Club of Switzerland

Lloyd's Yacht Club

Medway Yacht Club

Royal Air Force Yacht Club

Royal Bermuda Yacht Club

Royal Channel Islands Yacht Club

Royal Cornwall Yacht Club

Royal Cruising Club

Royal Dart Yacht Club

Royal Dutch Motorboat Club

Royal Dutch Rowing and Sailing Club 'De Maas'

Royal Dutch Sailing and Rowing Club

Royal Dutch Watersport Club 'De Kaag'

Royal Fowey Yacht Club

Royal Harwich Yacht Club

Royal Lymington Yacht Club

Royal Norfolk and Suffolk Yacht Club

Royal North Sea Yacht Club

Royal Ocean Racing Club

Royal Southampton Yacht Club

Royal Southern Yacht Club

Royal Ulster Yacht Club

Royal Welsh Yacht Club

Royal Windermere Yacht Club

Royal Yacht Squadron

Sussex Yacht Club

Single yacht club burgees in alphabetical order

Antigua Yacht Club

Bruxelles Royal Yacht Club

Cercle de la Voile de Paris

Clube Internacional de Regatas

Clyde Cruising Club

Coral Reef Yacht Club

Cruising Club of America

Cruising Yacht Club of Australia

Düsseldorfer Yacht Club, Germany

Eastern Yacht Club, USA

Fremantle Sailing Club

Gamla Stans Yacht Sällskap, Sweden

Golden Gate Yacht Club, USA

Göteborgs Kungl. Segel Sällskap

Household Division Yacht Club

House of Lords Yacht Club

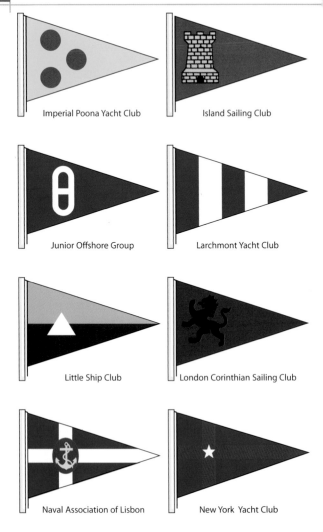

Imperial Poona Yacht Club

Island Sailing Club

Junior Offshore Group

Larchmont Yacht Club

Little Ship Club

London Corinthian Sailing Club

Naval Association of Lisbon

New York Yacht Club

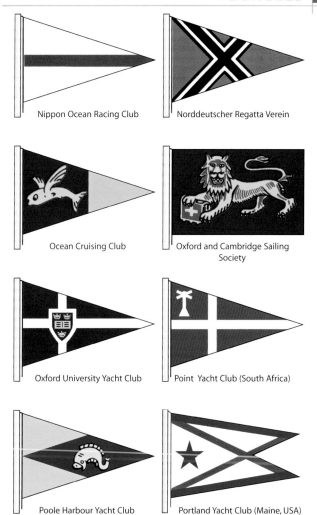

Nippon Ocean Racing Club

Norddeutscher Regatta Verein

Ocean Cruising Club

Oxford and Cambridge Sailing Society

Oxford University Yacht Club

Point Yacht Club (South Africa)

Poole Harbour Yacht Club

Portland Yacht Club (Maine, USA)

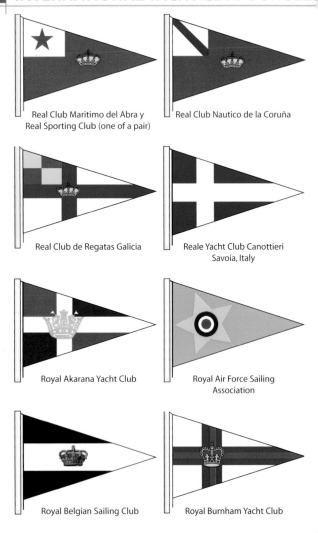

Real Club Maritimo del Abra y Real Sporting Club (one of a pair)

Real Club Nautico de la Coruña

Real Club de Regatas Galicia

Reale Yacht Club Canottieri Savoia, Italy

Royal Akarana Yacht Club

Royal Air Force Sailing Association

Royal Belgian Sailing Club

Royal Burnham Yacht Club

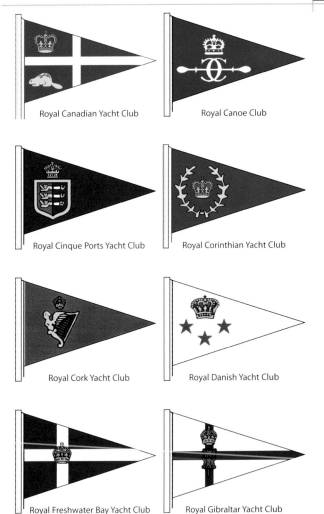

Royal Canadian Yacht Club

Royal Canoe Club

Royal Cinque Ports Yacht Club

Royal Corinthian Yacht Club

Royal Cork Yacht Club

Royal Danish Yacht Club

Royal Freshwater Bay Yacht Club

Royal Gibraltar Yacht Club

Royal Hawaiian Ocean
Racing Club

Royal Hong Kong Yacht Club

Royal Irish Yacht Club

Royal Largs Yacht Club

Royal London Yacht Club

Royal Malta Yacht Club

Royal Natal Yacht Club

Royal Naval Sailing Association

Royal New Zealand Yacht Squadron

Royal Northumberland Yacht Club

Royal Nova Scotia Yacht Squadron

Royal Norweigan Yacht Club

Royal Perth Yacht Club

Royal Port Nicholson Yacht Club

Royal Prince Alfred Yacht Club

Royal Swedish Yacht Club

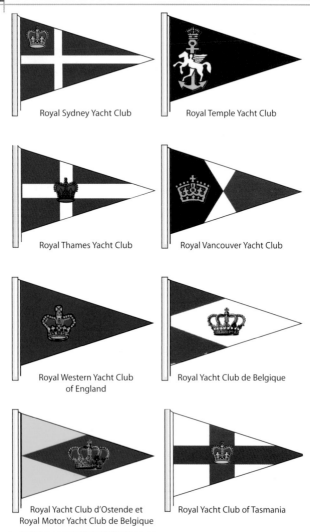

Royal Sydney Yacht Club

Royal Temple Yacht Club

Royal Thames Yacht Club

Royal Vancouver Yacht Club

Royal Western Yacht Club
of England

Royal Yacht Club de Belgique

Royal Yacht Club d'Ostende et
Royal Motor Yacht Club de Belgique

Royal Yacht Club of Tasmania

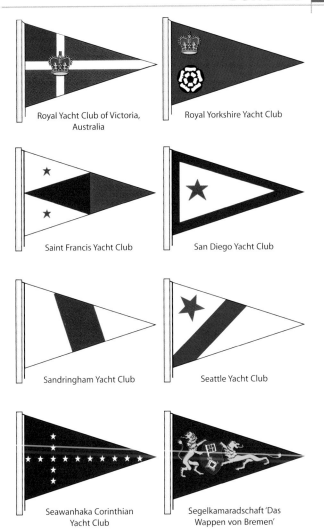

Royal Yacht Club of Victoria, Australia

Royal Yorkshire Yacht Club

Saint Francis Yacht Club

San Diego Yacht Club

Sandringham Yacht Club

Seattle Yacht Club

Seawanhaka Corinthian Yacht Club

Segelkamaradschaft 'Das Wappen von Bremen'

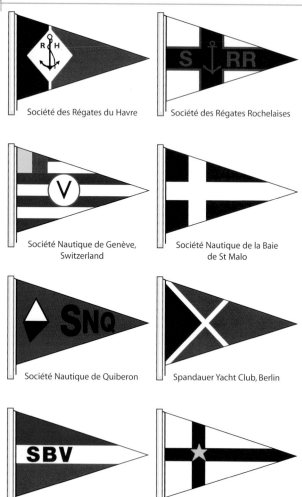

Société des Régates du Havre

Société des Régates Rochelaises

Société Nautique de Genève, Switzerland

Société Nautique de la Baie de St Malo

Société Nautique de Quiberon

Spandauer Yacht Club, Berlin

Sportbootvereiniging

Starcross Yacht Club

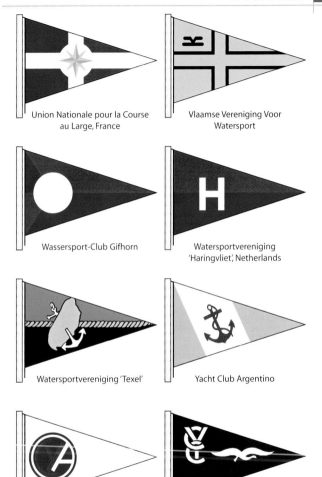

Union Nationale pour la Course au Large, France

Vlaamse Vereniging Voor Watersport

Wassersport-Club Gifhorn

Watersportvereniging 'Haringvliet', Netherlands

Watersportvereniging 'Texel'

Yacht Club Argentino

Yacht Club d'Arcachon

Yacht Club de Cherbourg

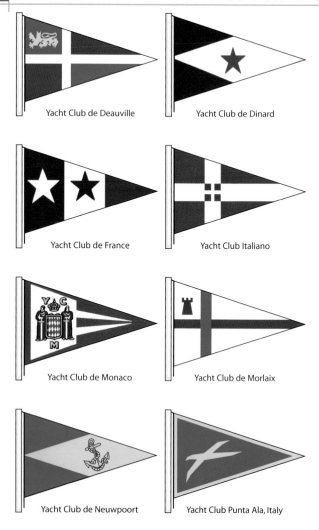

Yacht Club de Deauville

Yacht Club de Dinard

Yacht Club de France

Yacht Club Italiano

Yacht Club de Monaco

Yacht Club de Morlaix

Yacht Club de Neuwpoort

Yacht Club Punta Ala, Italy

NATIONAL MARITIME FLAGS

Albania

Algeria

Angola

Antigua and Barbuda

Argentina

Aruba

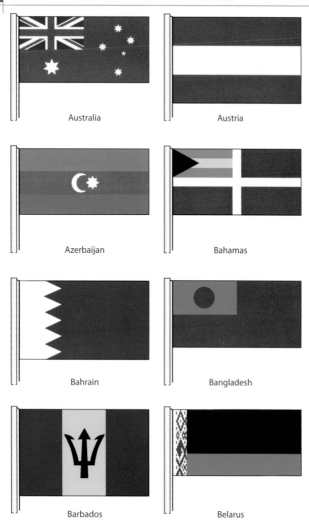

Australia

Austria

Azerbaijan

Bahamas

Bahrain

Bangladesh

Barbados

Belarus

Belgium

Belize

Benin

Bermuda

Bolivia

Bosnia and Herzegovina

Brazil

British Virgin Islands

Brunei Darussalam

Bulgaria

Cambodia

Cameroon

Canada

Cape Verde

Cayman Islands

Chile

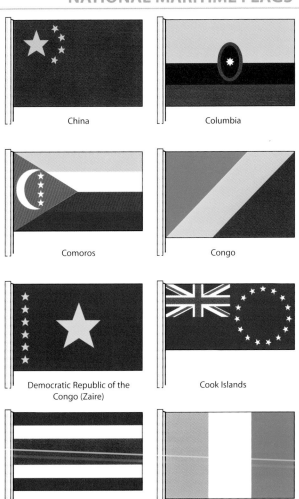

China

Columbia

Comoros

Congo

Democratic Republic of the
Congo (Zaire)

Cook Islands

Costa Rica

Côte d'Ivoire

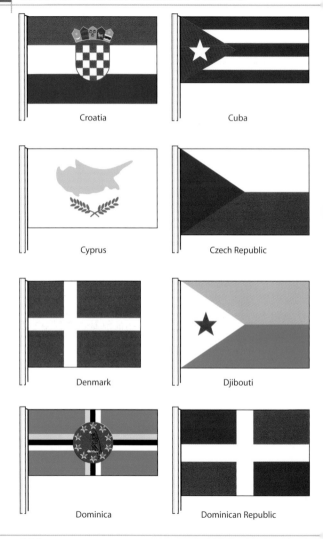

Croatia

Cuba

Cyprus

Czech Republic

Denmark

Djibouti

Dominica

Dominican Republic

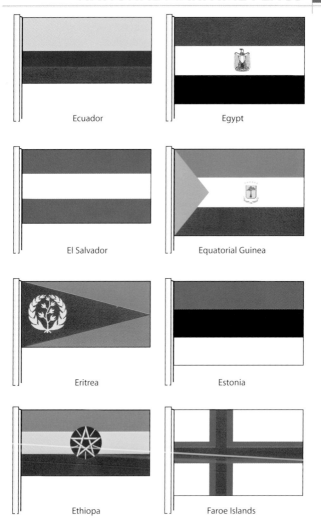

Ecuador

Egypt

El Salvador

Equatorial Guinea

Eritrea

Estonia

Ethiopa

Faroe Islands

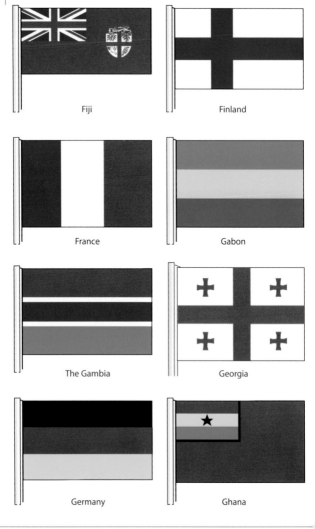

Fiji

Finland

France

Gabon

The Gambia

Georgia

Germany

Ghana

Gibraltar

Greece

Greenland

Grenada

Guatamala

Guernsey
(for use in coastal waters)

Guinea

Guinea-Bissau

Guyana

Haiti

Honduras

Hong Kong

Hungary

Iceland

India

Indonesia

Iran (Islamic Republic of)

Iraq

Ireland

Isle of Man
(for use in coastal waters)

Israel

Italy

Jamaica

Japan

Jersey

Jordan

Kenya

Kiribati

Democratic People's Republic
of Korea

Republic of Korea (South)

Kuwait

Latvia

Lebanon

Liberia

Libyan Arab Jamahiriya

Lithuania

Luxembourg

Macao

Macedonia

Madagascar

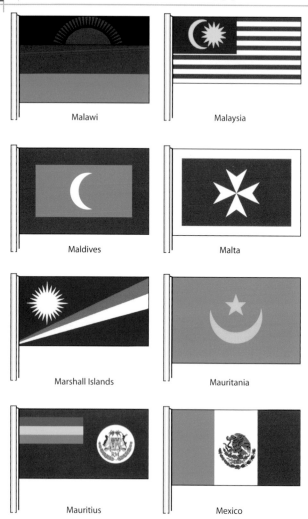

Malawi

Malaysia

Maldives

Malta

Marshall Islands

Mauritania

Mauritius

Mexico

Micronesia

Moldova

Monaco

Mongolia

Morocco

Mozambique

Myanmar

Namibia

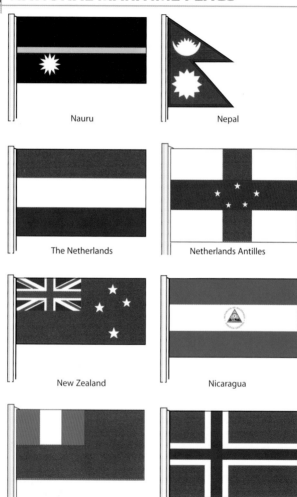

Nauru

Nepal

The Netherlands

Netherlands Antilles

New Zealand

Nicaragua

Nigeria

Norway

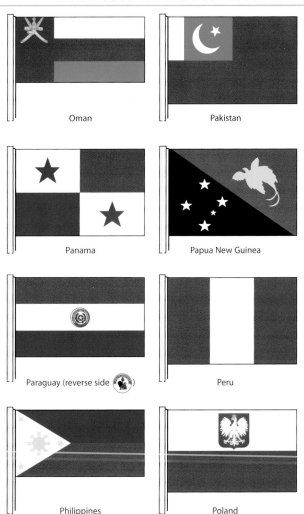

Oman

Pakistan

Panama

Papua New Guinea

Paraguay (reverse side)

Peru

Philippines

Poland

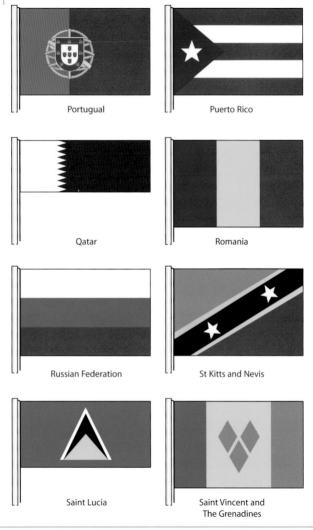

Portugal

Puerto Rico

Qatar

Romania

Russian Federation

St Kitts and Nevis

Saint Lucia

Saint Vincent and
The Grenadines

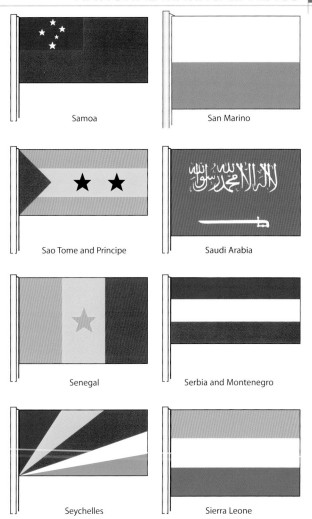

Samoa

San Marino

Sao Tome and Principe

Saudi Arabia

Senegal

Serbia and Montenegro

Seychelles

Sierra Leone

Singapore

Slovakia

Slovenia

Solomon Islands

Somalia

South Africa

Spain

Sri Lanka

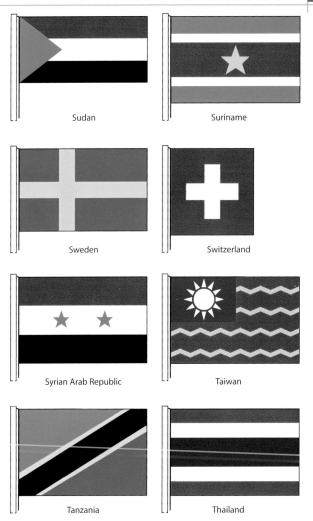

Sudan

Suriname

Sweden

Switzerland

Syrian Arab Republic

Taiwan

Tanzania

Thailand

Togo

Tonga

Trinidad and Tobago

Tunisia

Turkey

Turkmenistan

Turks and Caicos Islands

Tuvalu

Ukraine

United Arab Emirates

United Kingdom of Great Britain and Northern Island

United States of America

Uruguay

Vanuatu

Venezuela

Vietnam

Yemen

International flags

United Nations Organisation*

North Atlantic Treaty
Organisation (NATO)*

European Union*

*Not recognised as a maritime flag but may be flown unofficially with a
national ensign

GLOSSARY OF TERMS

Aft At the back end of a vessel

Almanac Annual diary containing tidal data and other statistical and astronomical data.

Aloft In the air, up in the rigging.

Answering pennant Used to acknowledge a signal, denote a decimal point, or indicate that the international code flags are in use and not naval signals.

Badge Emblem

Bermudan rig Single mast with tall, tapering, fore and aft, triangular sails.

Block Pulley.

Bowline Specific knot for marine use.

Breadth The short side of a flag.

Bunting A term for flags and other colourful festive decorations.

Burgee A triangular flag (pennant), usually with a yacht club logo, denoting membership of a specific club.

Canton Upper left hand corner of a flag, ie against top section of the hoist.

Civil ensign A maritime ensign for civilian use, usually undefaced.

Class association burgee A burgee denoting membership of a particular class.

Club association burgee see Burgee

Colours Another term for nautical flags.

Courtesy ensign A small version of maritime ensign of a foreign country flown by a visiting vessel.

Crosstrees A pair of horizontal poles designed to keep rigging from collapsing inboard.

GLOSSARY OF TERMS

Defacement, **defaced by** A badge, device or logo imposed on the design, by way of embellishment.

Device Another term for logo or emblem.

Dimension The long side of a flag also called the 'length'.

Dip salute see Salute

Dress overall, to To decorate a vessel with a full set of the International Code flags along with burgees and ensigns during celebrations.

Ensign A rectangular flag, flown on vessels to represent, and indicate, their nationality.

Evening colours, at Lowering time for ensigns and flags.

Field General background of the flag.

Flag officers A naval term used in yacht clubs denoting rank of certain officials, i.e. commodores, etc.

Fly The outer section of a flag which flaps freely.

Foot The bottom edge of a flag.

Fore and aft sails Modern design sails running from front to back of vessel as opposed to across her.

Fouled anchor An anchor symbol with line entwined around it.

Freeboard Side of a vessel's hull above the waterline.

Gaff Specific pole on head of a squared off mainsail or foresail (but not jib) to maintain sail shape.

Gaff-rigged A vessel having a mainsail (and foresails, but not jib) with a squared off head with a spar to maintain its shape.

Half mast Position on flagstaff or halyard, one third down from top.

Half-masting The ensign, and/or burgee, is raised and then dropped one third in recognition of a death.

Halyard A line for raising and lowering sails or flags.

Head The top edge of a flag.

Hoist The inner, short side of a flag, against the staff or halyard.

House flag A personal flag relating to the owner of the vessel.

Inglefield Clip A fastening used for securing flags.

International Code of Signals A set of flags each with an individual meaning, internationally recognised.

Jack A small flag flown only on the bow, (mostly naval use).

Jackstaff A rod in the bow of a vessel for the jack.

Ketch Two-masted vessel, the aft mast being smaller than the main mast and located in front of the rudder stock.

Laid up A flag which is no longer in use, but remains on display, is said to be 'laid up'.

Leech The back edge of a sail.

Make, to Alternative wording for hoisting a flag.

Maritime ensign A form of national flag specifically designed for maritime use.

Mooring An object secured to the sea or river bed to which in turn a boat may be tethered.

Morning colours, at Hoisting time for ensigns and flags.

Naval code flags An alternative set of code flags used by navies of NATO countries, different from the International Code of Signals flags.

Pennant A triangular flag.

Pilot jack The Union flag with a white border flown on jackstaff.

Port The left-hand side of vessel when looking forward from the stern.

Royal standard A flag or banner with the royal coat of arms, flown by royalty.

Salute, to To dip the ensign two thirds of the way down its staff or halyard and raise again.

Semaphore A message system using hand-held flags.

GLOSSARY OF TERMS

Seniority of positions The order of rank of importance of hoisted positions.

Schooner Two- or multi-masted vessel with the aftermost mast being taller than, or equal to, the foremast(s).

Sheave A wheel or turning block allowing movement of a line.

Spar Loose term for a yard, boom or mast.

Spreaders More modern version of crosstrees.

Staff Pole or rod from which to fly a flag.

Starboard The right-hand side of vessel when looking forward from the stern.

Strike, to To lower the flag.

Substitutes Three pennant flags (called repeaters in US) denoting repetition of previous flag in a signal.

Swallowtail, swallow-tailed Denoting shape – A rectangular flag with a V section cut out of the fly, which is also sometimes tapered.

Topmast Additional mast above main mast on a gaff-rigged vessel.

Triatic stay A wire that runs from the top of the main mast to the top of another mast; as on ketches, yawls, and schooners.

Undefaced A plain ensign, no logo.

Union canton The Union flag incorporated into left hand upper section (the canton) of a maritime ensign, or other flag.

Union flag, British A rectangular flag representing the Union of Great Britain and Northern Ireland. Shows the crosses of St George, St Andrew and St Patrick.

Vexillology A term denoting the study of flags, derived from Latin vexillum.

Yard Wooden pole for maintaining shape of a sail, usually on square sails

Yardarm Outer end of a yard.

Yawl Two-masted vessel, the aft mast being smaller than the main mast and located aft of the rudder stock.

APPENDIX 1

Yacht clubs using a special ensign

White ensign
Royal Yacht Squadron

Blue ensign
Royal Albert Yacht Club
Royal Brighton Yacht Club
Royal Cinque Ports Yacht Club
Royal Cruising Club
Royal Dorset Yacht Club
Royal Engineer Yacht Club
Royal Geelong Yacht Club
Royal Gourock Yacht Club
Royal Highland Yacht Club
Royal Marines Sailing Club
Royal Melbourne Yacht Club
Royal Motor Yacht Club
Royal Naval Sailing Association
Royal Naval Volunteer Reserve
   Yacht Club
Royal New Zealand Yacht
   Squadron
Royal Northern & Clyde Yacht
   Club
Royal Perth Yacht Club of
   Western Australia
Royal Port Nicholson Yacht Club
Royal Queensland Yacht Club
Royal Scottish Motor Yacht Club
Royal Solent Yacht Club

Royal South Australia Yacht
   Squadron
Royal Southern Yacht Club
Sussex Motor Yacht Club
Royal Sydney Yacht Squadron
Royal Temple Yacht Club
Royal Thames Yacht Club
Royal Western Yacht Club of
   England
Royal Western Yacht Club of
   Scotland
Royal Yacht Club of Tasmania
Royal Yacht Club of Victoria

**Blue ensign defaced by
club badge**
Aldeburgh Yacht Club
Army Sailing Association
Bar Yacht Club
City Livery Yacht Club
Cruising Yacht Club of Australia
Royal Air Force Yacht Club
Royal Akarana Yacht Club
Royal Anglesey Yacht Club
Royal Armoured Corps Yacht
   Club
Royal Artillery Yacht Club
Royal Australian Navy Sailing
   Association

Royal Bermuda Yacht Club
Royal Bombay Yacht Club
Royal Burnham Yacht Club
Royal Channel Islands Yacht Club
Conway Club Cruising Association
Royal Corinthian Yacht Club
Royal Cornwall Yacht Club
Royal Dee Yacht Club
Royal Forth Yacht Club
Royal Freshwater Bay Yacht Club
    of Western Australia
Royal Gibraltar Yacht Club
Royal Harwich Yacht Club
Royal Hong Kong Yacht Club
Household Division Yacht Club
Royal Irish Yacht Club
Royal Jamaica Yacht Club
Little Ship Club
Little Ship Club (Queensland
    Squadron)
Royal Lake of the Woods Yacht
    Club
Royal London Yacht Club
Medway Cruising Club
Royal Malta Yacht Club
Royal Mersey Yacht Club
Royal Motor Yacht Club of New
    South Wales
Royal Nassau Sailing Club
Royal North of Ireland Yacht Club
Royal Northumberland Yacht Club
Royal Ocean Racing Club
Parkstone Yacht Club
Royal Plymouth Corinthian Yacht
    Club

Poole Yacht Club
Royal Prince Alfred Yacht Club
Royal Prince Edward Yacht Club
Severn Motor Yacht Club
Royal Southampton Yacht Club
Sussex Yacht Club
Royal Suva Yacht Club
The Cruising Association
The House of Lords Yacht Club
The Medway Yacht Club
The Poole Harbour Yacht Club
Thames Motor Yacht Club
Royal Torbay Yacht Club
Royal Welsh Yacht Club
Royal Yorkshire Yacht Club
Old Worcesters Yacht Club

Red ensign defaced by club badge

Brixham Yacht Club
Royal Dart Yacht Club
Royal Fowey Yacht Club
House of Commons Yacht Club
Lloyd's Yacht Club
Royal Hamilton Amateur Dinghy
    Club
Royal Lymington Yacht Club
Royal Norfolk & Suffolk Yacht Club
Royal St George Yacht Club
St Helier Yacht Club
Royal Victoria Yacht Club
Royal Windermere Yacht Club
Royal Yachting Association
West Mersea Yacht Club

APPENDIX 2

Selected two-code signals

AC I am abandoning my vessel

AF I do not intend to abandon my vessel

AG You should abandon your vessel as soon as possible

AH You should not abandon your vessel

AL I have a doctor on board

AM Have you a doctor on board

AN I need a doctor

BR I require a helicopter urgently

CB I require immediate assistance

CK Assistance is not/or no longer required by me

CP1 SAR aircraft is coming to your assistance

DV I am drifting

DX I am sinking

IN I require a diver

IT I am on fire

JG I am aground. I am in a dangerous situation

JG1 I am aground. I am not in danger

	KJ I am towing a submerged object
	KJ1 I am towing a float
	KJ2 I am towing a target
	KK Towing is impossible under present weather conditions
	KL I am obliged to stop towing temporarily
	KM I can take you in tow
	KQ Prepare to be taken in tow
	KR All is ready for towing
	YG You do not appear to be complying with the Traffic Separation Scheme
	T1 You should navigate with caution. You are drifting towards my set of nets
	NB There is fishing gear in the direction you are heading
	NG You are in a dangerous position
	PD You should maintain your present course
	PP Keep well clear of me
	UL All vessels should proceed to sea as soon as possible owing to danger in port
	RZ1 You should not proceed out of harbour/anchorage
	CS What is the name or identity of your vessel (or station)
	VF You should hoist your identity signal

EF SOS/MAYDAY has been cancelled

LO I am not in my corrrect position (to be used by a light vessel)

PI You should maintain your present course

QO You should come alongside

QP I will come alongside

QR I cannot come alongside

QT You should not anchor. You are going to foul my anchor

RA My anchor is fouled

RN My engines are out of action

RO1 My propeller is fouled by hawser or rope

RO2 I have lost my propeller

SQ You should stop or heave to

UM The harbour or port is closed to traffic

UN You may enter habour immediately

UO You may not enter harbour

UW I wish you a pleasant journey

VJ Gale is expected from direction indicated (Complements Table III)

VK Storm is expected from direction indicated (Complements Table III

APPENDIX 3

Useful flag websites

The Flag Institute – www.flaginstitute.org
Flags of the World - www.flagspot.net
Burgees - www.burgees.com
World Flag Database - www.flags.net
Royal Yachting Association - www.rya.org.uk
Cruising Association - www.cruising.org.uk

APPENDIX 4

Overseas territories, departments, crown dependencies, or special administrative regions

American Samoa (USA)
Anguilla (UK)
Aruba (Neth) p. 99
Ascension Island (UK)
Ashmore and Cartier
    Islands (Aus.)
Baker island (USA)
Bassas da India (Fra.)
Bermuda (UK) p. 101
Bouvet island (Nor.)
British Antarctic
    Territory (UK)
British Indian Ocean Territory

British Virgin Islands (UK) p. 101
Cayman Islands (UK) p. 12, 102
Christmas island (Aus.)
Clipperton Island (Fra.)
Cocos (Keeling Islands) (Aus.)
Cook Islands (NZ) p. 12, 103
Coral Sea Islands (Aus.)
Dronning Maud Land (Nor.)
Europa island (Fra.)
Falkland Islands (UK)
Faroe Islands (Den.) p. 105
French Guiana
French Polynesia

INDEX

INDEX

INDEX